THE
INCREDIBLE CORAL REEF

ANOTHER ACTIVE-LEARNING BOOK FOR KIDS

Toni Albert

Illustrated and designed by
Ada Hanlon

Trickle Creek Books

"Teaching Kids to Care for the Earth"
500 Andersontown Road
Mechanicsburg, PA 17055

Acknowlegments.

Thank you, Bob Albert. Without you there would be no books!

Thanks, Pat Van Etten, for your unflagging enthusiasm for "teaching kids to care for the earth" and for your invaluable help.

Thank you, Linda Daniels, for helping me make friends with my computer.

Thank you, Joe Strykowski and Daphne Fautin, for scrutinizing the manuscript and for teaching me more about coral reefs.

Thanks, Ada!

Dedication.

To the incredible coral reefs of the world and to those who love them.

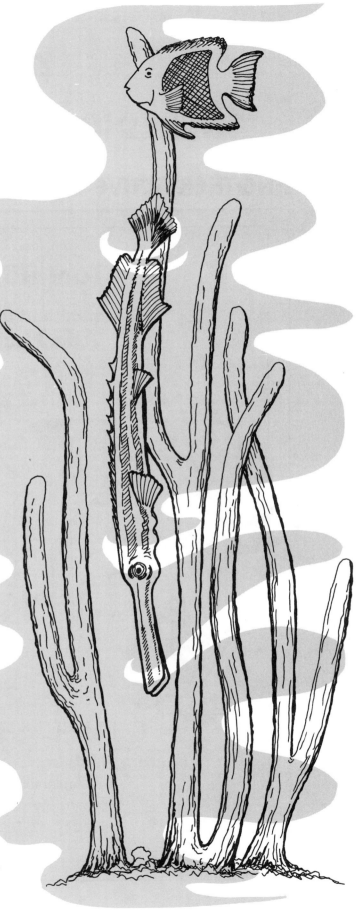

Publisher's Cataloging in Publication
(Prepared by Quality Books Inc.)

Albert, Toni.
    The incredible coral reef: another active-learning book for kids/
Toni Albert; illustrated and designed by Ada Hanlon.
    p. cm.
    Includes bibliographical references.
    SUMMARY: Covers the ecology of coral reefs, how they are
threatened and what kids can do to save them.
    ISBN 0-9640742-1-4
    1. Coral reef ecology--Juvenile literature. 2. Coral reef biology--
Juvenile literature. I. Title.

QH541.5.C7A53 1996   574.5'26367
                                          QBI96-20103

Library of Congress Catalog Card Number: 96-60150

Published in the United States by Trickle Creek Books
500 Andersontown Road, Mechanicsburg, PA 17055

CONTENTS

In the vast oceans that cover most of our planet, there are special places where the water is warm and clean and almost as transparent as air. Over millions of years, little flowery creatures called coral polyps have built massive reefs of rock on the skeletons of their ancestors. The coral reefs are riddled with crevices, tunnels, caves, and holes, which provide homes for an incredible variety of undersea wildlife.

The coral reef community is like a merry-go-round with gaudy colors, bold patterns, and crazy shapes. Around and around, in and out of the corals, neon-colored reef fish dart from point to point. Bright branches of fuzzy soft corals sway in electric-blue water; purple sea fans confront the current; yellow sponges house popping pistol shrimp. Sharks hover in the shadows of coral caves, and razor-toothed barracudas cruise silently above. Rays fly through the water with rippling wings. Rare sea turtles paddle and play.

The reef community is densely populated with hundreds and hundreds of marine animals and plants linked together in fascinating relationships. Day and night, there is busy activity on the reef, a complicated dance of feeding, competing, chasing, hiding, flirting, courting, mating, producing young, defending, attacking, and cooperating. The coral reef is more than a magical, colorful place. It is a whole system—one of the most important and diverse ecosystems on earth.

A thriving coral reef appears to be a solid mass of concrete-like rock, but it is surprisingly fragile. A fierce storm can break the coral into bits, or a change in current can smother the coral animals in mud. Natural predators eat the coral polyps. Sponges, algae, worms, and others burrow and bore into the coral until it breaks and falls as rubble on the seafloor. But throughout their ancient history, coral reefs have survived the blows inflicted by nature. The really devastating blows have been caused by human beings.

We have polluted and poisoned the clear water needed by coral reefs. We dredge up great chunks of coral to use in construction; we drag anchors and heavy nets across the delicate living polyps; we frantically overfish; we collect coral and shells and tropical fish with no thought for tomorrow. Many of the world's coral reefs are no longer lively, brilliant oases in the sea. They are diminished, dying, or dead.

We must act quickly to care for the incredible coral reef.

REEF REPORT

I learned to snorkel as a child when my family lived in Florida. I loved to swim in the ocean and ride the waves, but most of all, I liked to go snorkeling over the coral reef. It was like exploring another world, a fairyland under the sea—full of the strangest creatures and the most outlandish shapes and colors.

Later, as a young adult, I lived on the island of Maui in Hawaii. Then I snorkeled almost every day. The reef became as familiar to me as my own neighborhood. I knew exactly where to find a large moray eel peering out of his crevice with his mouth gaping and shutting, or where to look for sea urchins or mushroom coral or cowrie shells.

Even after I moved to Pennsylvania and became landlocked, I continued to visit the coral reef in my dreams. The magical images of the reef fish and the colored coral and the strange creatures had so impressed me that they never left me.

Sometimes my husband and I have traveled to parts of the world where we could visit the coral reef again, and the images are renewed. I'm always so grateful to find myself in the tropical sea again, swimming through schools of butter yellow fish that part to let me pass and then close ranks behind me. And I smile because I know I will see the fish again—in a technicolor dream.

WHERE IN THE WORLD ARE CORAL REEFS?

Coral reefs—like rainforests—are found inside a broad belt that circles the earth, stretching out on either side of the **equator**. Coral reefs are found in warm, shallow seas, often on the eastern shores of continents (where there are warm currents) or around small **tropical** islands. Reefs don't usually grow where the water temperature is below 20°C (68°F).

CORAL REEFS OF THE WORLD

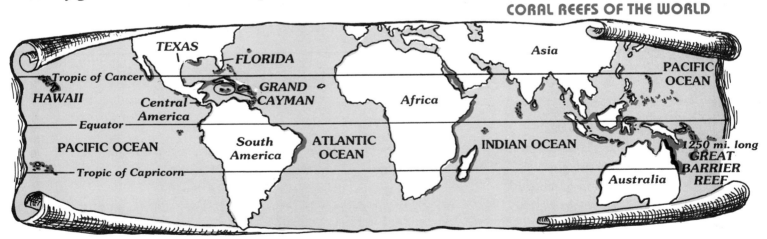

Note to Readers:
If you see a word in **bold type** like this, you can find the word in the glossary on page 60 or 61.

See if you can locate **(a)** Grand Cayman, where the author did the research for this book, **(b)** the coral reef nearest your home, **(c)** Australia's Great Barrier Reef, the longest barrier reef in the world. (How long *is* it?)

REEF REPORT

When I considered where to complete the research for this book, I chose Grand Cayman in the West Indies for a special reason. Not only are the Cayman Islands recognized as one of the most beautiful diving and snorkeling places in the world, but there is a site in the North Sound of Cayman Bay where people can swim with stingrays! The Southern Stingray, with its giant "wings" and dangerous venomous spine near the base of its powerful tail, has become tame enough to feed and pet.

I told my husband, "Kids will love to read about swimming with stingrays!"

He smiled at me with a knowing look.

"I'm just thinking of our readers," I said. But my heartbeat was already quickening with anticipation.

We flew over the Florida Keys and Cuba on our way to Grand Cayman. Then suddenly we saw the small islands below us, and there were the stunning, characteristic colors of the sea where coral reefs grow. The colors ranged from an unbelievable swimming-pool turquoise to deep indigo. I couldn't wait to get in the water and meet those stingrays!

CORALS ARE PARTICULAR ABOUT WHERE THEY LIVE

Corals are living animals that must have specific conditions in which to grow. Reef-building corals have tiny single-celled **algae** living inside their bodies, and the algae need sunlight in order to produce food. So reef builders grow in clear, shallow, sun-drenched water. (They grow best in water less than 30 feet deep.) The best reef building occurs in warm water that remains between 74 and 78°F. Corals live in water that is poor in nutrients, such as phosphorous, ammonia, and dissolved nitrates, and poor in **phytoplankton**, or tiny plant life, too. The water is a startling clear blue, reflecting the blue of the sky, because there is so little microscopic green algae in it.

Try This! . . . Make a Wave Bottle

What You Will Need:
- A clear plastic bottle
- White vinegar
- Blue and green food coloring
- Vegetable oil
- Heavy tape, such as duct tape or electrical tape

What to Do:
1. Remove the labels from a clear plastic bottle, such as a small soft drink bottle.
2. Fill the bottle half full of white vinegar.
3. Add drops of blue and green food coloring until you create a stunning tropical color.
4. Fill the bottle to the very top with vegetable oil. Squeeze the bottle to remove any air bubbles.
5. Screw the lid on the bottle and secure it with heavy tape.

Make waves by rocking the wave bottle from side to side!

REEF REPORT

As soon as we arrived, we made arrangements to take several chartered boat trips later in the week—one to swim with the stingrays, of course! We also planned to see the "coral gardens" on the barrier reef and explore two sunken wrecks! In the meantime, we wanted to spend our first few days on the island getting reacquainted with the coral reef.

Within an hour of our arrival on Grand Cayman, we were in the water. Our hotel wasn't located on the beach. It was built on rock, the "iron shore," and the ocean surged against the rock not far from our room. The strange underwater world of the coral community was as close as a single jump into the water. I jumped!

At first I saw such a collision of colors and shapes that I didn't know where to look. I swam quickly, knowing that behind every coral head, there would be some new discovery. The water was fifteen or twenty feet deep with long sandy corridors between outcroppings of coral.

Brightly colored fish swam through liquid sparkles, and everything around me was interesting.

But gradually I began to focus more and more closely on what I was seeing: little spiny sea urchins in every crevice; rocks covered with green and blue algae; swaying fingers of soft coral; small green sea fans; and a six-inch green Fireworm. (I was careful not to touch the worm. Its glasslike bristles can cause pain for hours.) I looked carefully at the fish around me and identified them with a fish card. We didn't leave the water until dinnertime.

Many of the best places to snorkel are close to shore. In this scene, big-eyed Squirrelfish hide under coral crevices.

REEF ZONES

Different kinds of corals thrive in various areas of the coral reefs where they have adapted to different conditions of sunlight and wave action. Reef scientists have divided the reef into zones to help them study it. (The zones vary in reefs around the world.) The **reef crest** is the shallowest—and sunniest—part of the reef, where waves break. Boulder corals and Elkhorn corals live there. Light-loving corals may be found in the

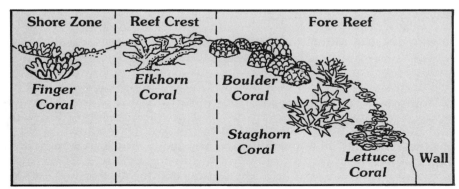

REEF ZONES

shore zone when the water is shallow and sediment-free. In the deep water and dim light of the fore reef, corals become flattened to capture as much sunlight as possible. Off the Cayman Islands, a shelf of coral ends in a vertical wall that plummets thousands of feet down!

Animal, Vegetable, or Mineral?

Coral reefs are massive, rocklike structures of limestone. Think of the Great Barrier Reef stretching more than a thousand miles along the coast of Australia. What is coral? Is it a nonliving rock? Think of the soft corals with fuzzy branches swaying with the surge of the ocean. They look like a field of underwater wildflowers. What are these corals? Are they plants?

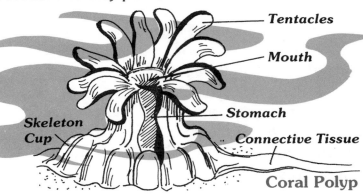

Tentacles
Mouth
Stomach
Connective Tissue
Skeleton Cup
Coral Polyp

Corals are living animals! The individual animals are called **coral polyps**. Most polyps are smaller than a pea, but some kinds grow to be more than 30 centimeters (1 foot) in diameter. The polyp looks something like a sea anemone. It has stinging tentacles surrounding its mouth, and a hollow cavity, closed at one end, that serves as its stomach.

A reef-building coral polyp continually secretes a hard, cup-shaped skeleton around itself. The cup is made of calcium carbonate, like limestone. Many reef-builders are **colonial**. Thousands of individual polyps are connected together by a film of living tissue, which extends over the surface of their combined skeletons. As the coral colony grows, new polyps build cup skeletons on top of the old ones. Gradually, the skeletons build up into huge coral rocks, and together, the coral rocks make up a coral reef. Miles of reef and tons of rock are produced by billions of tiny coral polyps!

Connected Polyps

Try This! Play "Animal, Vegetable, or Mineral?"

Play a reef guessing game with your family or friends. The person who is "it" must think of something that is part of the reef community and ask the other players to guess what it is. The other players begin by asking, "Is it animal, vegetable, or mineral?" The person who is "it" might answer, "Animal," if the answer were a fish or a crab—or even if the answer were a sponge or a sea anemone! Remember, reef animals are tricky to identify. "It" would answer, "Vegetable," if the answer were a plant, such as algae or turtle grass. He or she would answer, "Mineral," if the answer were nonliving, such as sand or seawater. The other players then take turns asking the person who is "it" questions. The questions can only be answered with "yes" or "no." When a player thinks he or she knows the answer, the player can ask a direct question, such as, "Is it a moray eel?" If the answer is "no," play continues. If the answer is "yes," the player who guessed correctly becomes "it."

OR ALL THREE?

Scientists call coral polyps animals, but living coral tissue actually includes a plant! Tiny one-celled algae, called **zooxanthellae**, live inside the polyps. This tight partnership between animal and plant is the foundation of reef life. Working together, the polyp and algae can accumulate and recycle nutrients in clear tropical water where nutrients are scarce. The zooxanthellae trap energy from the sun and produce food through **photosynthesis**. The polyp captures tiny animals floating in the water with its tentacles. Then the algae and the polyp exchange various compounds to benefit them both. And somehow, their partnership produces the limestone that serves as the polyp's skeleton cup—a feat that neither one could accomplish alone. So you see, corals can't be simply defined as animal, vegetable, or mineral, because they combine elements of all three!

Directions: Now that you know something about coral polyps, see if you can solve some coral reef mysteries. *Answers are on page 62.*

1. Why do corals need to live in shallow water that receives plenty of sunshine? _____
   _____

2. If coral polyps are mostly transparent, what do you think gives them their colors? (Corals are often tans or greenish-browns.) _____
   _____

3. The coral polyp and its algae both benefit from living together. The polyps obtain food and oxygen; the algae obtain shelter and fertilizer from the polyps' waste products. Do you know what this kind of close relationship is called? _____
   (*If you need help, see page 27.*)

Soft corals often look like plumes and plants. They are supported by flexible rods of protein or small spikes of calcium carbonate instead of rigid skeletons. When they die, they leave no lasting skeletons. Soft coral polyps have 8 tentacles with little side projections like feathers, and they are often extended during the daytime.

Hard corals, the reef-builders, look like rocks during the day, when each polyp is withdrawn into its skeleton cup. At night when the polyps are feeding, the coral is fuzzy and colorful with thousands of tiny waving tentacles. Hard corals have 6 or more tentacles, but never 8 tentacles.

CORAL AS PREY—AND PREDATOR!

You might think that coral polyps would be safe inside their deep skeleton cups, but they are prey to many enemies. Hordes of urchins, worms, snails, mussels, sponges, sea stars, and fish eat coral tissue and bore into the reef. The Parrotfish bites off chunks of coral, swallowing the polyps and expelling fragments of skeleton. The Green Reef Crab simply plucks the polyps from their cups.

When polyps are eaten, an area of white skeleton is exposed, and algae or sponges may settle there. Or other animals may take the opportunity to bore into the coral and attack from within. Boring sponges, mollusks, and sea urchins actually change the shape of the reef by weakening and breaking the coral. Coral colonies will even attack each other when they are competing for space.

Corals Can Be Mean

Coral polyps don't have to find plants to eat; they cultivate algae in their own bodies. During the day, while the algae produce a garden of food through photosynthesis, the polyps are withdrawn into their skeleton cups. You might say the coral functions as a plant during the day. But at night, the tiny coral polyps extend their tentacles and become some of the most efficient predators in the sea. At night, they function as predatory animals!

How can a tiny, stationary, flower-like animal be a predator? A colony of polyps, with all their waving tentacles, present a living wall of mouths and stinging tentacles. When **zooplankton**, tiny drifting and floating animals, are carried by water currents over the reef, almost all of them are devoured. And the coral polyps get their share.

Zooplankton include tiny fish, fish eggs, jellyfish, larvae, copepods, krill, and microscopic animal life. Most of the zooplankton drift helplessly wherever the current takes them. When zooplankton brush against the tentacles of coral polyps, they trigger an explosion of stinging darts, called **nematocysts**. The zooplankton are captured and swept into the polyps' mouths. Once the food is digested, it can travel throughout the coral colony to other polyps.

Try This!

If you live near the ocean or visit the ocean, collect some seawater in a jar. Take it to school and ask if you can look at it under a microscope. Look for plankton, the microscopic plants and animals in the water. Or pull a sheer "knee-high" stocking through ocean water to see what tiny critters you can catch. Maybe you will catch a copepod, one of the most numerous animals in the sea.

Copepod

A Life Cycle That Goes Round . . . and Round

If you are confused about whether a coral polyp is an animal, a vegetable, or a mineral, wait until you try to make sense of its life cycle! At times, a polyp grows by budding, almost the way a tree does. At other times, it produces eggs and sperm the way animals do.

In the Pacific Ocean, a perfectly timed event is triggered by the full moon. Once a year (or for some corals, once a month), hundreds of different species of corals release a snowstorm of eggs and **sperm** together. The eggs, like tiny seeds, are fertilized by the sperm and become floating baby corals called **planulae**. These little larvae are less than one-thousandth of an inch long. They are covered with tiny waving hairs that enable them to swim slowly through the water. Each planula feeds on plankton and swims from place to place until it finds a suitable spot to settle. It may take hours or months for the planula to find a hard surface where the water is clean and clear. The wave action, the temperature, and the light must be just right!

Once the planula is settled, it begins to build the stony cup that will anchor it to the bottom. And it changes into a coral polyp. This little polyp is the first member of a new coral colony. New polyps form by **budding**—by branching from the first polyp much as a bud sprouts from the side of a tree. The buds grow larger until they separate from the original polyp and form their own skeleton cups. As the budding continues, the coral colony increases in size.

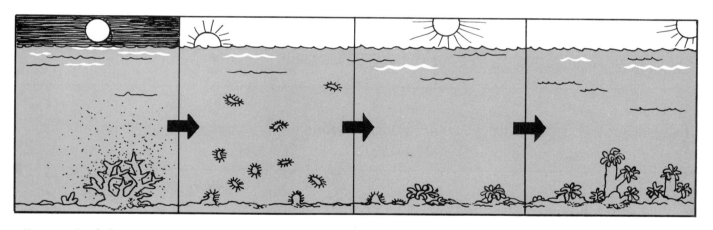

During the full moon, many corals release eggs and sperm.

The tiny fertilized eggs become planulae.

When the planula settles, it changes into a polyp.

The coral polyp forms more polyps by budding.

Corals have lived on earth for millions of years. Do you think it has helped them to have *two* ways of producing new polyps? When polyps are produced by budding, a single polyp can cover a rock with a colony of polyps. The only problem is that all of the polyps belong to a **clone**, a group of individuals that are identical to the first polyp. If the colony is threatened by a change in the environment, all of the polyps will be in equal trouble. When polyps grow from planulae, each polyp is different from the others and each establishes a different colony. If several colonies are threatened by a change, they will respond in different ways and some of the colonies will probably be able to survive.

CONSIDER THE KINDS

Kindly consider the kinds of coral-colored corals
that careless collectors collect in common colanders.

There are hundreds of different **species**, or kinds, of corals. Each species builds its skeleton in a unique way and grows in a particular pattern. Corals can be round or flat or branched. They can look like mushrooms, deer horns, flowers, or brains! Each species can usually be identified by its shape and form.

Directions: The common names of corals are very descriptive. See if you can fill in the names of the corals that are not labeled in the illustration. Use the clues given below to help you, and choose the names from the Word Bank. *Answers are on page 62.*

1. This coral can form six-foot-high mounds. Its name sounds like something you would like to have.
2. This is one of the few hard corals that has polyps that may be active during the day. (Most polyps in hard corals hide in their skeleton cups during the day.) This coral looks like part of a person's hand reaching up from the bottom of the sea.
3. Small clumps of this beautiful coral are often found at the base of a large boulder. The coral looks like it is growing on short stalks.
4. This is the most common coral in the Caribbean. It looks like a big rock.
5. Brightly colored fireworms attack this coral at night. They eat the tips of its delicate branches, which look like deer antlers.

WORD BANK				
Flower Coral	Boulder Coral	Thick Finger Coral	Staghorn Coral	Giant Brain Coral

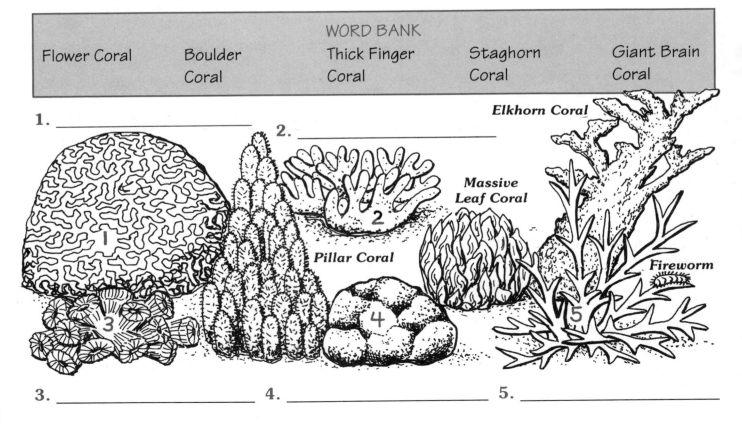

1. _____

2. _____

Elkhorn Coral

Massive Leaf Coral

Pillar Coral

Fireworm

3. _____   4. _____   5. _____

Make a Magical Coral Reef

A wonderful way to learn about the coral reef is actually to build one! You can make a coral reef community with clay, paper, and colored markers. Don't forget to add imagination, information, creativity, and color!

What You Will Need:
   A large unbreakable jar with a wide mouth and a lid
   Sand
   Modeling clay or Play-Doh®
   Very small branches from a shrub or tree
   Toothpicks
   Heavy drawing paper
   Colored markers
   Nylon thread
   Tape

Some Other Things You Might Use, Too:
   Seashells or macaroni shells
   Plastic canvas (used for cross-stitch)
   A real sponge or synthetic sponge
   Yarn

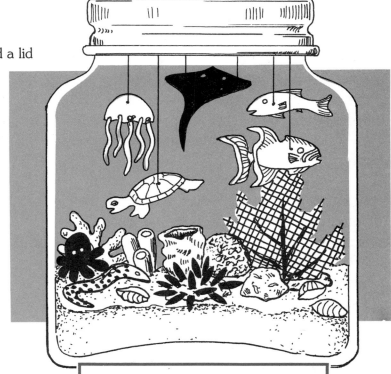

See "Sea Art" on pages 52 and 53 for art ideas.

What to Do:

1. Choose a large jar with a wide mouth, so that you can get your hand into the jar. Make sure the jar has a lid. Pour an inch or two of sand into the bottom of the jar.

2. Use different colors of modeling clay or Play-Doh® to make different kinds of **corals**. Remember that corals can be branching, plate-like, or mounded. Mold clay around a small branch from a shrub to make a branching coral. Use a toothpick to etch its "design" on the surface of each coral. For example, Brain Coral has deep, wavy grooves.

3. Carefully arrange your clay corals on the sand in the bottom of your jar.

4. Draw several **fish** on heavy drawing paper and cut them out. Color the fish on both sides with colored markers. Use bright colors and bold designs. With a toothpick, make a small hole at the top of each fish. Tie a length of nylon thread to each fish, and tape the other end of the thread inside the jar lid, so that the fish are suspended over the coral when the lid is on the jar.

5. Create a **stingray, sea turtle**, or other sea animal out of paper, too. Attach *two* lengths of thread to the stingray to keep it in a "flat" position. Make a paper **jellyfish** with yarn tentacles.

6. Use clay to make an **octopus, sea star,** or **moray eel.** Make a **sea urchin** out of a small ball of clay. Paint half-toothpicks black or red and stick them into the clay for spines.

7. Cut a **sea fan** from a small piece of plastic canvas. Color it on both sides with markers and stand it up in a base of clay.

8. Scatter bits of **sponge** and **seashells** or decorated macaroni shells on your magical coral reef.

REEF REPORT

There are many places to snorkel and dive off Grand Cayman that are within swimming distance of the shore, but several times we went to special sites by boat. One day we traveled across the wide North Sound to reach an incredibly beautiful area of "coral gardens." I stood in the bow of the boat looking across the sun-dappled water to the horizon. I could see a white line of surf where the waves from the open ocean were breaking over the outer reef.

After the boat was anchored in a sandy-bottomed Turtle Grass bed, we swam away from it against a strong current. That way, as we snorkeled over the reef, we would be swept back toward the boat. The boiling surf and the shallow, turbulent water made it hard to maneuver over the coral. We had to be very careful not to grab coral for a handhold or damage it with our fins.

Gardens of coral thrive in this violent environment. Soft corals sway and bend dramatically in the surging sea. Sea fans position themselves perpendicular to the current, so that they can catch the plankton that sweeps into them. The purple or green sea fans, swaying back and forth, look like lacy fans held by invisible women of another century. Elkhorn coral in three colors survive the battering waves and shelter schools of bright fish.

The colors and fierce movement were dizzying, but oh! how I loved it!

On the outer reef, soft corals sway with the current while fish face the current.

THE CORAL REEF ECOSYSTEM

The coral reef **ecosystem** often includes a delicately balanced marine environment of **mangrove** swamps, sea grass beds, and coral reefs. All of these areas are like a close family; they are tightly related and dependent on each other.

The Mangrove Swamp

Mangrove trees grow in coastal wetlands where the water is a mixture of salt water and fresh water. A tangle of roots rise like stilts above the water or grow down into the water from overhead branches. The roots of mangrove trees, twining together, form a net that traps eroded soil and **pollutants** and slows the flow of fresh water into the sea. The maze of roots also provides a nursery where young fish and other sea animals find food and shelter until they are big enough to live on the reef. The mangrove swamps stand as a natural defense against the winds and waves of hurricanes.

The Sea Grass Bed

The calm water between the shore and a reef is called a **lagoon**. The sandy lagoon is often an underwater meadow of Turtle Grass and other sea grasses. The sea grass beds act as huge filters that remove particles that wash from land into the sea. They help keep the water over the reef clear and clean. Countless fish and other sea life graze on the sea grasses and find shelter from hungry predators there. Sea grass beds are important nurseries for the young of many species. Sea grasses release oxygen into the water, too, and their roots keep the sandy bottom from moving and changing.

Directions: Answer the question that follows. Circle the letter in front of the answer you choose. Then look at the illustration of a coral reef ecosystem at the bottom of the page. Label the mangrove swamp, the sea grass bed, and the coral reef. *Answers are on page 62.*

1. What happens to the coral reef when mangrove swamps are cleared or filled and sea grass beds are disturbed?

   (A) The coral is poisoned by pollution. **(B)** Dirt muddies the water and smothers the coral. **(C)** There is no place for juvenile reef fish to find shelter and food. **(D)** All of the above. **(E)** None of the above.

(a) _____ (b) _____ (c) _____

REEF REPORT

At some of the most popular shallow reefs, the fish have become tame and beg for handouts. Some divers offer them canned cheese, which is squirted like toothpaste underwater. The reef fish swarm together to feed and the water boils with darting, dancing fish of every color. Sometimes the fish were so crowded around me that I couldn't see past them, and I felt as if I were being stirred in a thick fish soup.

It's fun to see so many fish at once, but feeding the fish disturbs their natural feeding patterns and encourages them to depend on divers for food. Because their natural behavior is changed, they become easy prey for fishermen and more vulnerable to natural predators, too.

I prefer to "fish-watch" in a quieter way. I like to float motionless above the reef and look at one fish at a time. What is its shape and size and color? What is it *doing*? I carry a "Fishwatcher's Field Guide" in the water. It's a plastic card with colored pictures of fish and their correct names. Often, when I hold the card to look at it, curious fish come close enough to nibble the edges of the card—or even my fingers. So while I'm examining the fish, they're examining me!

Sometimes I carry an underwater notebook too, so that I can make notes about what I see. Then when I return home, I can read my smeary, wobbly notes and remember!

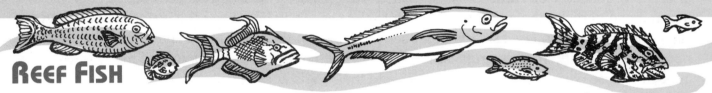

REEF FISH

Most of the tropical sea is a watery desert where marine life is scarce. But coral reefs are brimming with life. There are more fish there than anywhere else in the sea. More than 100 different species of fish have been identified on an area of reef about 10 feet in diameter! On a single reef (perhaps 100 acres in area), 400 or 500 species may be found.

The striped fish are black and yellow Sergeant Majors, the fish with big eyes are red Squirrelfish, and the slim fish are yellow and blue French Grunts.

How can so many fish survive together on the reef? If all the fish were competing for the same food in the same way at the same time of day, they *couldn't* survive. The reason they can share the reef is that each one fits into a special **niche** that is different from that of its neighbors. There are nighttime feeders and daytime feeders. There are fish that eat plankton, corals, algae, sea animals, little fish, or big fish. There are fish that are farmers, grazers, or hunters. There are fish that can eat sea urchins, hard corals, or parasites inside a big fish's mouth!

REEF REPORT

I enjoyed renting a really fine underwater camera. The camera and a strobe light were mounted on the ends of a foot-long bar, so I needed both hands to hold it and could only swim with my feet. The first time I used the camera, I looked around underwater and everywhere I looked was so beautiful, I decided I couldn't go wrong. I would dive down, point the camera in any direction, and expect a great photo.

I especially enjoyed the angelfish. Two of them were swimming with me, as tame and gentle as puppies, when suddenly a little neon missile hit my face mask. It was a Yellowtail Damselfish,

a small black fish with bright blue spots and a butter-yellow tail. When I positioned the camera to take its picture, the fearless little fish attacked the camera!

I looked around to see what valuable piece of real estate this feisty damselfish was defending. I saw a coral head below me with dime-sized white scars where the damselfish had nibbled on the living coral. When algae grows on the bare spots, the damselfish eats the algae. This little gardener ferociously drives away any plant eater that enters its territory. (How did it know that I like salad?)

Try This! Make a Fish Print

What You Will Need:
   A fresh fish
   A paper towel
   Newspaper
   Clay
   Straight pins
   Paint
   Paper

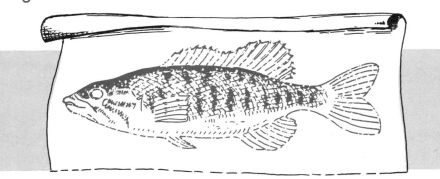

You can make a shell print, too!

What to Do:
1. Use a fish you have caught yourself. Or if you buy a fish from a market, choose one with clear eyes, bright red gills, and a fresh smell.
2. Wash the fish carefully with soap and water. Then dry it with a paper towel.
3. Place the fish on a layer of newspaper. Spread the fins out and pin them to clay that has been mounded to the height of the fish's body, so that the fins will show up in the final print.
4. Paint the fish with one or more colors of tempera paint or water colors.
5. Place a sheet of paper over the fish and press it gently against the fish's body and fins. Remove the paper and look at your fish print!

I thought I knew what a parrotfish looked like—like a parrot, of course! I had seen parrotfish with the glorious blues and greens of a tropical bird and with a "beak" of fused teeth like a parrot's beak. But I was surprised by the parrotfish's changing wardrobe. Parrotfish wear completely different outfits, depending on their species, age, and sex.

The first Stoplight Parrotfish I saw wore a brown and white checkered coat with a red vest, but the next one (a **supermale** that was once a female) wore a shimmering cloak of blues, greens, pinks, and purples. The Queen Parrotfish wears either drab grayish-black or a rainbow of blue, green, pink, and yellow. A young Blue Parrotfish flaunts blue and brown stripes, but the adult dresses all in blue. The Midnight Parrotfish wears a gown of deep blue velvet.

In spite of their confusing costumes, you can tell they are all members of the same family. Their teeth give them away. They have strong crunchers designed to grind up coral along with the algae that they like to eat. I spent hours following parrotfish as they grazed. They are a delight for the eyes and, surprisingly, for the ears too. I could actually hear them crunching underwater!

Directions: To see some of the parrotfish's varied costumes, color the fish below. **B**=**blue**, **Br**=**brown**, **G**=**green**, **Gr**=**gray**, **O**=**orange**, **P**=**purple**, **Pi**=**pink**, **R**=**red**, **W**=**white**, **Y**=**yellow**

THE PARROTFISH

During the day, a parrotfish uses its powerful, beak-like jaws to crunch on solid coral rock. The parrotfish eats the coral polyps and algae growing on the coral. In the fish's throat, there is a kind of "mill" that grinds the chunks of coral into a fine white powder. After the algae is digested, the powder is expelled in a white cloud. Scientists have estimated that for every acre of reef, one ton of coral rock is changed into fine sand every year—mostly by parrotfish.

As twilight approaches, the parrotfish stop feeding, fall into formation like a line of marching ants, and swim into deeper water to spend the night. Each fish settles into a nook or crannie and, unlike most other fishes, falls into a deep sleep. The parrotfish produces a mucus **cocoon** around itself to prevent predators from finding it by smell. In the morning, the cocoon is left behind, and the parrotfish returns to eating algae and making sand.

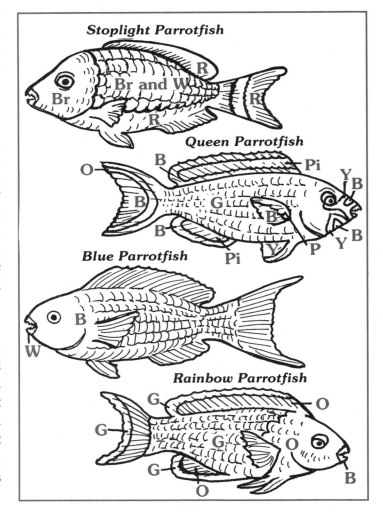

Stoplight Parrotfish

Queen Parrotfish

Blue Parrotfish

Rainbow Parrotfish

REEF REPORT

On a bright sunshiny day, sunlight penetrates the shallow water over the reef, and the result is dazzling. The reef and its creatures are dappled with shimmering points of light and shadow. But on a stormy day when the waves are high and the light is dim, the reef has an entirely different look.

Early one morning, the sky was overcast and the sea was rolling with great swelling waves. I entered the water with difficulty from a rocky shore. When the water rose to the top of the rock, I dove in on the crest of a wave and immediately fell with the water, so that the rock was high above my head. The waves were alarming and I felt like a cork bobbing wildly up and down, up and down.

I swam out into deeper water—about twenty feet deep—so that I wouldn't be battered against the rocks and coral. Below me, coral heads rose like ghosts out of a sandy mist. The water was murky and violent.

Suddenly, as if from nowhere, a long slender fish appeared in front of me and then hung motionless in the gray water. It was big, at least four feet long, and I could see its teeth. This was the Great Barracuda! For a few moments we didn't move except with the rocking of the waves. Then like a silver bullet, it shot into deeper water, leaving me breathless.

THE GREAT BARRACUDA

On many reefs, where sharks come and go, the Great Barracuda is the top predator. With its tremendous stealth and speed, it can catch almost anything. Small fish are swallowed whole, while larger fish like grunts and snappers are chopped neatly in half with a snap of powerful jaws and sharp pointed teeth.

Sometimes the Great Barracuda hunts like a lone wolf, hovering with chilling stillness until it suddenly strikes with stunning speed. At other times, barracudas seem to hunt in packs. Even young barracudas, growing up among mangroves and sea grasses, are formidable predators.

The Great Barracuda can grow to be six feet long. Its slender body is built for speed and its coloring is designed for hunting. The barracuda's usual barred silver pattern provides perfect **camouflage**, making it difficult to see. The fish can alter its colors to enable it to blend into any background. In a grass bed, the barracuda looks like a shiny mirror. In darker surroundings, the fish adopts an olive-green pattern. Resting over sand, the barracuda is a pale white and gray.

It is extremely rare for a person to be attacked by a Great Barracuda unless the fish is provoked (for example, by a spearfisher). Like all predators, the barracuda has a particular size of prey, and a person is too big to trigger its feeding patterns. Thank goodness!

REEF REPORT

Another eerie experience is seeing the wreck of a sunken ship resting on the bottom of the sea. We went by boat to see the wreck of the Cali, a steel-hulled ship that was caught in a hurricane. Thirty-foot waves slammed the hull against the bottom until it cracked. Water seeped in and soaked the cargo, which happened to be a load of rice. The wet rice swelled until it broke the hull of the ship in half!

The wreck of the Cali lies in fairly shallow water, about fifteen feet deep, so it was easy to dive down for a closer inspection. How strange to find reef animals comfortably settled on the ruined steel structure. Corals, algae, and sponges grew on the ship's surface. I saw the clawless Spiny Lobster peering out of a crevice formed by bent metal. And near one end of the wreck, I spotted a pufferfish, who was too secure to puff up. (When threatened, a puffer can inflate its abdomen until it is two or three times its normal size.)

We also visited the Oro Verde, the most famous sunken ship on Grand Cayman. The Oro Verde was deliberately sunk as an artificial reef in 1980. A great community of reef fish lives there and divers love to observe them.

The Oro Verde lies fifty feet underwater. Something about the depth of the water and the slant of the afternoon sun made the water an electric blue. When I dove in, it was like entering a vat of deep blue dye! Far below me, I could see scuba divers exploring the wreck, and they looked like tiny dolls. I felt small, too, with so much ocean around me.

ARTIFICIAL REEFS

A sunken wreck, oil rig, or other manmade structure can offer protection to a wide variety of marine animals. A thriving reef community lives on the "artificial reef" in an otherwise barren environment.

Checkered Puffers

Is This a FISH TALE?

Yes or No?

It can be dangerous for reef animals to live on artificial structures.

Answer is on page 62.

THE REEF CONNECTION

Directions: Follow the directions at the bottom of the page for "making reef connections." Make the connections by drawing a line from one dot to another. You may draw more than one line from a single dot. The clues will help you. When you make all the connections, you will see an ARTIFICIAL REEF! *See page 62 for an illustration of the completed puzzle.*

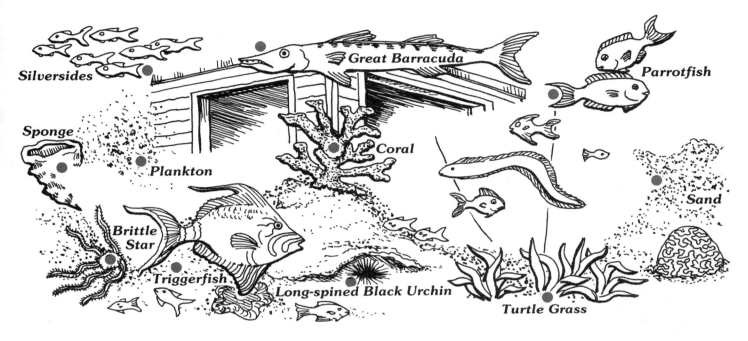

1. Draw a line from a mass of tiny animal and plant life to one of their predators. **CLUE:** The predator is a school of silver fish.
2. Draw a line from a school of small silver fish to one of their predators. **CLUE:** The predator is a slender fish with long pointed teeth.
3. Draw a line from an animal with five long spiny arms to a sea animal that provides its home. **CLUE:** The sea animal looks like a vase.
4. Draw a line from a sea animal that looks like a vase to its food. **CLUE:** The sea animal feeds on a mass of tiny animal and plant life.
5. Draw a line from a mass of tiny animal and plant life to another of their predators. **CLUE:** This predator is a colony of polyps.
6. Draw a line from a colony of polyps to a fish that eats them. **CLUE:** The fish has a strong "beak" that can crunch rock.
7. Draw a line from a fish with a strong "beak" to a fine substance that the fish expels. **CLUE:** The substance is ground up rock.
8. Draw a line from a substance that is ground up rock to a plant that grows in it. **CLUE:** The plant is an underwater grass.
9. Draw a line from an underwater grass to an animal that lives in and eats the grass. **CLUE:** The animal is covered with long spines.
10. Draw a line from an animal that is covered with long spines to a fish that is able to eat it. **CLUE:** The fish has beautiful markings.

REEF REPORT

I wanted to visit the Cayman Turtle Farm where thousands of Green Turtles are raised. The Turtle Farm was started in 1968 as a business to sell turtle meat and turtle shells worldwide. But ten years later, because sea turtles are endangered animals, the United States banned all turtle products from even passing through US ports. Then the Turtle Farm began to focus more on research and breeding programs. It helps scientists all over the world to understand more about sea turtles.

At the Turtle Farm, hundreds of sea turtles, from 2-ounce hatchlings to 600-pound adults, are kept in holding tanks. The turtles, which are given a continuous supply of fresh seawater and high-protein food, thrive and breed. The Turtle Farm is the only place where two generations of Green Turtle hatchlings have been hatched in captivity.

Visitors are allowed to handle some of the young turtles, so I had the unusual experience of catching and holding a little sea turtle. Sea turtles are not usually aggressive—they bite only what appears to be food—but I was surprised at how strong the turtle's front flippers were. I had to struggle to hold it securely.

What an irresistible little creature! Its shell was golden brown and perfectly patterned. Its head and flippers looked like a mosaic of tiny tiles. And its ivory-colored throat was the smoothest, finest leather, a delight to touch.

ENDANGERED SEA TURTLES

Today all sea turtles are threatened or endangered, but there was a time when they were plentiful. It's wonderful to imagine what the first explorers saw off the coasts of Florida, Georgia, and the Carolinas. When Columbus discovered the Cayman Islands on his last voyage, he wrote in his journal, "We were in sight of two very small and low islands, full of tortoises, as was all the sea about, insomuch that they look'd like little rocks." Columbus named the islands "Tortugas," or Turtles. Later they were renamed the Caymans.

During the seventeenth century, sailors from all nations came to the Caymans to take on live turtles to use for fresh meat. By the next century, the

It's fun to hold a baby Green Sea Turtle! Notice that it has flippers instead of feet. Sea turtles are helpless and clumsy on land but strong and graceful in the water.

Green Turtles were so rare that ships no longer came. Today theTurtle Farm has released more than 30,000 tagged sea turtles, so that swimmers can once again encounter them in the wild.

THE WORLD'S MOST VALUABLE REPTILES

Sea turtles, called "the world's most valuable reptiles," have long been valued for their meat, oil, shells, and skin. Unfortunately, they have almost been valued to death. Today, besides being overhunted to the brink of extinction, they are threatened in many other ways.

People use the sea turtle's nesting beaches for recreation or construction.

Hunters kill turtles and take turtle eggs from beaches for food.

Sea turtles drown in commercial fishing nets and shrimp nets.

Sea turtles are poisoned when they eat crabs or jellyfish that are full of chemicals from pollution in the ocean.

Sea turtles die when they eat plastic trash that litters beaches and oceans.

Sea turtles are killed to make luxury products, such as tortoiseshell combs, shoes and handbags, and stuffed turtles that are hung on walls.

Most nations of the world now have laws to protect sea turtles and their nesting sites. Sea turtle populations are slowly beginning to recover, although the Kemp's Ridley Turtle is still very close to becoming extinct.

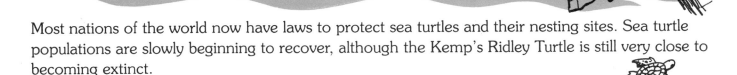

Try This! Adopt a Sea Turtle!

You can adopt a Loggerhead Turtle from the Caribbean Conservation Corporation, PO Box 2866, Gainesville, FL 32602 for $25. Or adopt a stranded sea turtle from the Okeanos Ocean Research Foundation, Inc., 431 East Main Street, Riverhead, NY 11901 for $18. Write for information.

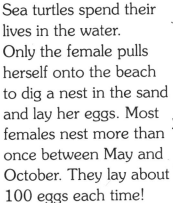

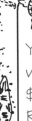

Sea turtles spend their lives in the water. Only the female pulls herself onto the beach to dig a nest in the sand and lay her eggs. Most females nest more than once between May and October. They lay about 100 eggs each time!

Many of the eggs are eaten by crabs, raccoons, and other animals. After about 60 days, the remaining eggs hatch, but it takes the hatchlings another two or three days to reach the surface of the sand. The tiny turtles weigh less than two ounces. Most of them are eaten by predators before they can reach the sea. Only one or two will survive from each nest.

ALIENS IN THE SEA

Some of the bizarre creatures that live on the coral reef are as unearthly as aliens from other galaxies. As marine scientists learn more about reef animals and plants, they uncover strange and mysterious facts. Even a simple sponge has remarkable secrets to reveal.

Directions: Read below about the sponge. Then in the box at the right, write about another reef animal of your choice. Here are some suggestions: a Moray Eel, a shark, a seahorse, a Spiny Lobster, a Scorpionfish, a Frogfish, a sea star, or an octopus.

SPONGE

A sponge is an animal that consists mostly of holes. It has no brain, heart, or nervous system. It cannot move or defend itself. Yet sponges have survived on earth for hundreds of millions of years without changing.

Sponges are very primitive animals with only a few kinds of cells, but many species of sponge have a characteristic shape. In an amazing experiment, a living sponge was mashed through a fine silk cloth. The separated cells rearranged themselves into a perfect copy of the original sponge!

Sponges seem to be immune to bacterial infection. At Yale University, a dead sponge was kept for more than five years without decaying. Sponges are an important source of new medicines.

Some sponges are living condominiums, which house tiny fish, shrimp, crabs, worms, brittle stars, and sea anemones.

THE REEF IS RIDDLED WITH . . .
RIDDLES

Directions: See if you can solve these riddles with the names of reef animals. If you need help, look for the answers in the illustration of the coral reef below. *Answers are on page 62.*

1. What do you call a coral that won an Oscar?

   _____

2. Why couldn't the sponge get a date?

   _____

3. What do you call a coral that speaks five languages?

   _____

4. What kind of cat has eight legs?

   _____

5. What kind of fish goes well with peanut butter?

   _____

6. What kind of person loves the sea?

   _____

7. What do you call a sponge that needs to do its laundry?

   _____

8. What kind of crab lives alone?

   _____

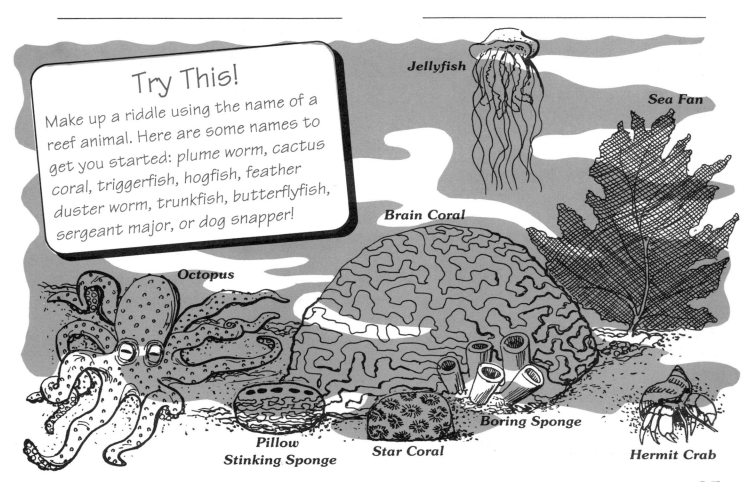

Try This!

Make up a riddle using the name of a reef animal. Here are some names to get you started: plume worm, cactus coral, triggerfish, hogfish, feather duster worm, trunkfish, butterflyfish, sergeant major, or dog snapper!

Jellyfish

Sea Fan

Brain Coral

Octopus

Boring Sponge

Pillow Stinking Sponge

Star Coral

Hermit Crab

JUST THE TWO OF US

The coral reef is crowded with a dense population of animals and plants, all competing for food or light and for living spaces and hiding places. Most members of the reef community are related to each other as **predators** or **prey**, but some live together in surprising symbiotic relationships!

Cleaning Stations

Some small fish such as Neon Gobies and Fairy Basslets, and certain shrimp such as Spotted Cleaning Shrimp and Barber Pole Shrimp, are **cleaners**. They feed on tiny **parasites** on big fish, which would ordinarily feed on *them*. Cleaners even go inside a fish's mouth to pick its teeth without being harmed. They pay special attention to fish with wounds or sores, giving them a thorough cleaning.

This truce between predators and prey is accomplished through elaborate body language. Cleaners set up **"cleaning stations"** where large fish wait in line to be groomed. The fish show that they want to be cleaned by posing, yawning, flaring their fins and gills, or even by standing on their heads or walking on their tails. The cleaning shrimp and cleaning fish indicate that they are willing to oblige by doing neat little "cleaner dances."

Try This!

Create a "Cleaner Cartoon" by writing what you think the grouper and goby are saying. Don't forget to sign your name at the bottom of the cartoon.

The cleaning shrimp rock from side to side, whipping their antennae like signal flags. The brightly colored cleaning fish perch on coral heads in an obvious way.

Gray Angelfish

Is This a FISH TALE?
A cleaner fish will pick at a diver's hand if the diver presents it to be cleaned.

Yes or No?

Answer on page 62.

At cleaning stations, both the cleaners and the cleaned are benefited. The cleaners get fed. Aren't they clever to enlarge their feeding grounds by feeding on the surfaces of fish! And the cleaned fish are freed of irritating parasites. In one study, when scientists removed all the cleaners from a small reef, most of the other fish left. The remaining fish had frayed fins and lots of parasites.

MORE TWOSOMES

The tight relationship between cleaning fish and the larger fish they clean is an example of **symbiosis.** *Symbiosis* literally means "living together." When two species live closely together, they may both benefit or only one may benefit or one may be harmed.

Directions: First read about the three kinds of symbiosis in the box below. Then, on this page and also on page 28, read about some of the strange partners that live on the reef. Decide which kind of symbiotic relationship they share. Circle your answer. *Answers are on page 62.*

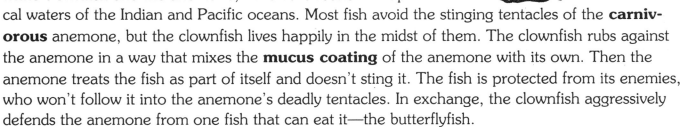

Clownfish and Sea Anemone

The Clownfish and the Anemone

Probably the most famous symbiotic pair is the orange and white clownfish and the anemone, which are found in tropical waters of the Indian and Pacific oceans. Most fish avoid the stinging tentacles of the **carnivorous** anemone, but the clownfish lives happily in the midst of them. The clownfish rubs against the anemone in a way that mixes the **mucus coating** of the anemone with its own. Then the anemone treats the fish as part of itself and doesn't sting it. The fish is protected from its enemies, who won't follow it into the anemone's deadly tentacles. In exchange, the clownfish aggressively defends the anemone from one fish that can eat it—the butterflyfish.

1. This is an example of **(a) mutualism, (b) commensalism, (c) parasitism.**

The Isopod and a Reef Fish

An isopod is a small **crustacean**, a little bit like a shrimp. Some isopods attach themselves with tiny sharp claws to a fish. Their mouthparts pierce the fish's skin, so that they can feed on its blood and tissue fluids. The isopod often holds onto the fish's head near its eyes or mouth and may damage the fish's skin and bone structure, but the fish will continue to feed and go about its business. The two may live together for a long time.

2. This is an example of **(a) mutualism, (b) commensalism, (c) parasitism**.

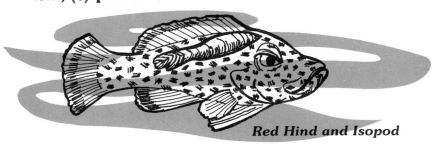

Red Hind and Isopod

Kinds of Symbiosis

 Mutualism: a relationship between two species in which both benefit.

 Commensalism: a relationship between two species in which one benefits and the other is neither benefited nor harmed.

 Parasitism: a relationship between two species in which one benefits while the other is harmed.

HERMITS THAT AREN'T HERMITS

Hermit crabs must live their lives in hand-me-downs. Unlike other crabs, a hermit crab doesn't have a shell protecting the rear part of its body, so it adopts the empty shell of another creature—a snail. The hermit's body is so soft and flexible that it can fit into a shell of almost any shape, but eventually it will outgrow its borrowed shell and have to look for another. This process of eyeing every empty shell it comes across—and often trying it on for size—goes on throughout the hermit crab's life. Some hermits have even decided to live in coconut shells, soup cans, or pieces of bamboo. If you ever see a can of soup walking across the sea floor, you'll know what it is!

Directions: Read below about some hermit crabs that aren't hermits! (At least, they don't like to live alone.) Decide which kind of symbiotic relationship is described, and circle your answer. Refer to the box on page 27, "Kinds of Symbiosis," if you need to. *Answers are on page 62.*

The Star-Eyed Hermit Crab and the Tricolor Anemone

Certain hermit crabs, such as the Star-Eyed Hermit, attach sea anemones, especially Tricolor Anemones, to their shells for protection. Scientists have observed that the Common Atlantic Octopus is able to kill a hermit crab without anemones, but those with anemones always survive. The anemones sting the octopus, sending it scuttling away in pain. And what does the anemone get for its trouble? A free ride to good eating places and scraps from the hermit's dinner.

You can tell that both the hermit crab and the anemone are happy with their partnership, because either one may get the relationship started. The crab may tap and tickle the anemone until it lets go of whatever it is attached to, so that the crab can place the anemone on its shell. Or the anemone may reach out with its tentacles and hop aboard the crab's shell on its own.

Star-eyed Hermit Crab and Tricolor Anemone

3. This is an example of **(a) mutualism**, **(b) commensalism**, **(c) parasitism.**

The Spotted Porcelain Crab and the Red Hermit

The Spotted Porcelain Crab is a beautiful little crab less than an inch long. It is orange-red with white and lavender polka dots, and each dot is ringed with red. The tiny crab commonly shares a shell with a hermit crab, especially the Red Hermit, which is much the same color. (Do you see *both* crabs in the illustration at the right?) The porcelain crab gains protection and leftovers to eat, but the Red Hermit would probably be just as happy without its tiny roommate.

4. This is an example of **(a) mutualism**, **(b) commensalism**, **(c) parasitism.**

Spotted Porcelain Crab and Red Hermit

Is There a Crab in Your House?

Is there a crab in your house? (Don't count bad-humored family members.) If not, you might want to consider getting one. Land hermit crabs make great pets!

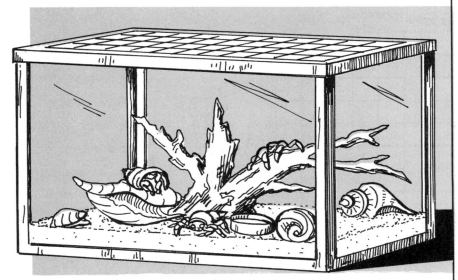

Try This!

The Spotted Decorator Crab is one of several crabs on the coral reef that is an "exterior decorator." It attaches bits of algae, sponges, and other encrusting organisms to its shell for camouflage. If the crab gets hungry, it can feed off its decorations! Try gluing pieces of moss, lichen, or wood (even sequins and beads) to an empty shell for your hermit crab. When it moves in, it will have the fanciest house in town!

How to Keep a Pet Hermit Crab

What You Will Need:

An aquarium with a tight lid
Sand or gravel
Landscaping materials

A water dish or a sponge
Dechlorinated water
Food

A spray bottle or mister
Clean, empty shells
One or more land hermit crabs

What to Do:

1. Prepare a home for your hermit crab by putting about 2 inches of sand in the bottom of an aquarium. The aquarium must have a tightly fitting screen top or lid. Landscape with clean driftwood, branches (especially decaying wood), rocks, or other materials for the crab to climb on. Be sure to provide a number of carefully cleaned shells that are a little larger than the one your hermit crab is living in.

2. Buy bottled water or evaporate the chlorine from tap water by letting the water sit out for 24 hours before giving it to your crab. Your hermit can drink from, and wade in, a heavy, shallow dish of water, or it can drink from a small wet sponge. Use a mister to spray your hermit with water several times a week.

3. Every other day, feed your hermit a small amount of "land hermit crab food" from the pet store. You can also give it corn meal, peanut butter, bits of fruits and vegetables, dog biscuits, etc. Remove any spoiled food immediately.

4. Your hermit crab will be comfortable at room temperatures from 65°F to 85°F. Don't place your pet near an air conditioner or heater.

5. In nature, hermits live in groups. You might want to have more than one hermit crab.

6. Little hermits can walk on your hand. Hold larger crabs by grasping their shells at the rear. Enjoy getting to know your hermit!

THE REEF IS A PUZZLE

Directions: Use words from the **blue** Word Bank to complete the crossword puzzle below. *Answers are on page 62.*

Word Bank

predator
lagoon
sponges
algae
protection
commensalism
mutualism
parasitism
plankton
reef
endangered
mangrove
parrotfish
symbiosis
dances
prey
stations
zones
shell
parasites

Across

2. The kind of symbiosis between coral and the algae living inside it.
5. The Kemp's Ridley Sea Turtle is the most ____.
6. What the Decorator Crab "decorates."
7. The relationship between isopods and fish.
10. The sandy area between the shore and the reef.
11. The relationship between the Spotted Porcelain Crab and the Red Hermit.
13. A fish that sleeps in a cocoon.
14. Fish line up at cleaning ____ to get rid of parasites.
16. The posing and posturing of cleaner fish.

Down

1. A shark.
2. A tropical tree growing along a low-lying coast.
3. A ridge of coral near the surface of the water.
4. Drifters in the ocean.
6. Living closely together.
7. A hermit crab acquires an empty shell for ____.
8. "Apartment houses" for shrimps, fish, worms, etc.
9. Cleaners remove tiny ____ from fish.
12. Different areas of the reef.
13. The animal that gets eaten.
15. Many fish graze on underwater pastures of ____.

PLAY
REEF PARTNERSHIPS

Number of Players: *Reef Partnerships* is a perfect game for two *partners,* but three kids can play, too. For four or more players, it is best to photocopy the cards to make a deck of 48 cards.

Object of the Game: To earn points by completing sets of cards. A complete set is 3 cards—a "partnership" card showing a symbiotic partnership between two reef animals and 2 "reef animal" cards showing each of the individual animals. Of course, another object of the game is to learn about some of the strange relationships between reef animals.

Directions: 1. Deal 6 cards to each player. Place the remaining cards facedown in a draw pile. Players must check their cards for "partnership" cards and place those cards faceup in front of them. During each turn, players do three things: play one card if possible, draw one card, and play or discard one card. *More directions on page 32.*

Neon Goby and Nassau Grouper

A cleaning fish, the Neon Goby, picks tiny parasites from a Nassau Grouper. Then the grouper feels better.

Neon Goby

Nassau Grouper

Tricolor Anemone and Star-Eyed Hermit Crab

A Star-eyed Hermit Crab attaches a Tricolor Anemone to its shell to discourage its enemies. And the anemone gets a free ride.

Tricolor Anemone

Star-Eyed Hermit Crab

Directions (continued):

2. A player plays a "reef animal" card by placing it faceup on the correct "partnership" card that is faceup. Then the player draws a card from the draw pile. If it is a "partnership" card, the card must be placed faceup in front of the player. If the card is a "reef animal" card, it can be played on anyone's "partnership" card or discarded on the discard pile. The player may choose to keep the card and discard another from his or her hand.

3. Anytime a player completes a set of three cards, no matter who they are in front of, the player takes the set, keeping the cards facedown. (Completed sets will earn points at the end of the round.)

4. When a player plays all of his or her cards, the player can choose to end the game by going out or to continue the game by taking one card from the draw pile. If the player stays in the game and draws a card, his or her turn ends without playing or discarding the card drawn. The card may be played at the next turn.

5. If the draw pile is used up, players can draw from the discard pile. If both piles are used up, each player in turn plays off the faceup "partnership" cards until one player goes out.

6. When a person goes out and chooses to end the game, points are counted: **10 points for going out - 20 points for each set you have completed - 5 points for every faceup card in front of you, including cards that other players have played on your "partnership" cards - 5 points subtracted for each card left in your hand.** The first player who earns 250 points wins. Four players may want to play to 500 points.

Man-of-War Fish and Portuguese Man-of-War Jellyfish

The Man-of-war Fish hide among the deadly tentacles of the Portuguese Man-of-war Jellyfish. The jellyfish are not benefited.

Man-of-War Fish

Portuguese Man-of-War Jellyfish

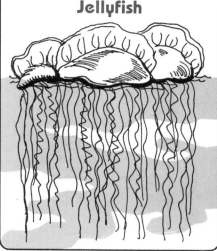

Snapping Shrimp and Orangespotted Goby

A Snapping Shrimp shares its burrow in the sandy mud of the sea floor with an Orangespotted Goby. The goby guards the entrance and alerts the shrimp to danger.

Snapping Shrimp

Orangespotted Goby

Colonial Anemones and Lavendar Tube Sponge

Bright yellow Colonial Anemones on a drab Tube Sponge warn fish away from the sponge. The sponge provides living space for the anemones.

Colonial Anemones

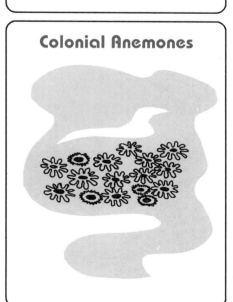

Lavendar Tube Sponge

Urchin Crab and Long-Spined Black Urchin

An Urchin Crab lives under the formidable spines of the Long-spined Black Urchin. The sea urchin doesn't receive anything in return for protecting the crab.

Urchin Crab

Long-Spined Black Urchin

Cleaning Shrimp and Spotted Moray Eel

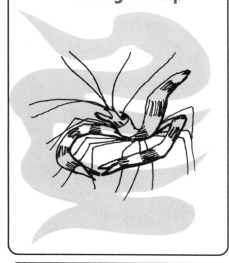

A Cleaning Shrimp finds tiny bits of food and trims unhealthy tissue from the Spotted Moray Eel. The shrimp gets a meal; the eel gets relief.

Cleaning Shrimp

Spotted Moray Eel

Conchfish and Queen Conch

During the day, a Conchfish hides in the mantle of a live Queen Conch. The Queen Conch is probably not benefited.

Conchfish

Queen Conch

WORDS OF WARNING

Directions: Read the list of words below the puzzle. Each word that is printed in **BLUE** is hidden in the puzzle. Circle the words as you find them. When you have circled all thirty words, the left-over letters will reveal "words of warning" about coral reefs. Read the message from left to right and from top to bottom. *Answer on page 62; message on page 63.*

```
S  I  C  O  R  A  L  N  C  E  A  S  T  I  N  G  R  A  Y  L
S  L  C  C  P  L  A  C  O  N  C  H  R  S  P  O  N  G  E  S
Q  T  L  T  S  G  L  A  G  O  O  N  O  U  F  B  T  H  E  R
U  E  E  O  E  A  P  L  A  N  K  T  O  N  F  Y  A  R  E  C
I  P  A  P  S  E  A  O  N  N  E  C  T  L  U  R  C  H  I  N
R  A  N  U  E  G  D  T  A  H  E  D  E  I  S  T  R  U  C  C
R  R  E  S  T  O  T  I  N  O  N  O  F  G  R  O  U  P  E  R
E  R  R  M  U  R  E  V  E  E  N  O  N  H  E  P  R  A  R  A
L  O  S  A  R  G  T  E  M  P  E  R  A  T  U  R  E  T  C  B
F  T  A  N  T  O  N  M  O  R  A  Y  C  A  U  S  E  E  A  S
I  F  C  G  L  N  O  M  N  P  L  A  N  G  E  L  F  I  S  H
S  I  E  R  E  I  T  E  E  C  D  A  M  S  E  L  F  I  S  H
H  S  H  O  B  A  R  R  A  C  U  D  A  A  N  G  E  I  N  T
H  H  E  V  E  N  N  J  E  L  L  Y  F  I  S  H  T  I  R  E
R  E  E  F  S  S  H  R  I  M  P  F  I  R  E  W  O  R  M
```

CORAL	SPONGES	ANEMONE	DAMSELFISH	JELLYFISH
ALGAE	SHRIMP	SEA Fan	FIREWORM	GORGONIANS
SUNLIGHT	CLEANERS	Sea URCHIN	CONCH	LAGOON
PLANKTON	PARROTFISH	STINGRAY	MORAY Eel	TURTLE Grass
TEMPERATURE	CRABS	GOBY	ANGELFISH	REEF
MANGROVE	BARRACUDA	SQUIRRELFISH	OCTOPUS	GROUPER

Message: _ _ _ _ _ _ _ _ _ _ _ _ _ _ _ _ _ _ _ _ _ _ _ _

_ _ _ _ _ _ _ _ _ _ _ _, _ _ _ _ _ _ _ _ _ _ _ _ _ _ _ _

_ _ _ _ _ _ _ _ _ _ _ _ _ _ _ _ _ _ _ _ _ _ _ _ _ _-

_ _ _ _ _ _ _ _ _ _ _ _ _ _ _ _ _ _ _ _ _ _ _ _ _.

THE DAY SHIFT

Day and night on the reef are like two different worlds. The reef animals that are active by day seek shelter in reef caves and crevices at night. And the reef animals that were hidden in those same crevices during the day emerge at night. When the day shift and the night shift change—in the morning and in the evening like clockwork—there is all the hustle and bustle and confusion of rush hour. And rush hour on the reef is more dangerous than the busiest highway, because twilight predators are cruising the reef looking for prey.

During the day, the polyps of hard corals are tightly closed, hiding in their skeleton cups. Even soft corals are "wilted" and shrunken in size. But beautiful reef fish, such as triggerfish, parrotfish, damselfish, butterflyfish, and wrasse, are actively feeding. In addition, some **nocturnal** fish, such as cardinalfish and squirrelfish, hover around the reef seeking shelter from predators like barracuda, which hunt by day.

TWILIGHT

Directions: Look at each reef animal illustrated on this page. Notice its number. Then find the same number on page 39 and draw a picture of the animal in the space provided. As you complete the illustration on page 39, you will find out how the reef changes from day to night.

During the twilight of dusk and dawn, some of the most ferocious predators on the reef hunt and kill. Sharks, jacks, groupers, and snappers prowl the reef, lunging upward when they see their prey outlined against the waning light. These twilight predators don't belong to the day shift or the night shift. They hunt and sleep around the clock, killing most of their prey in the gray twilight rush hours.

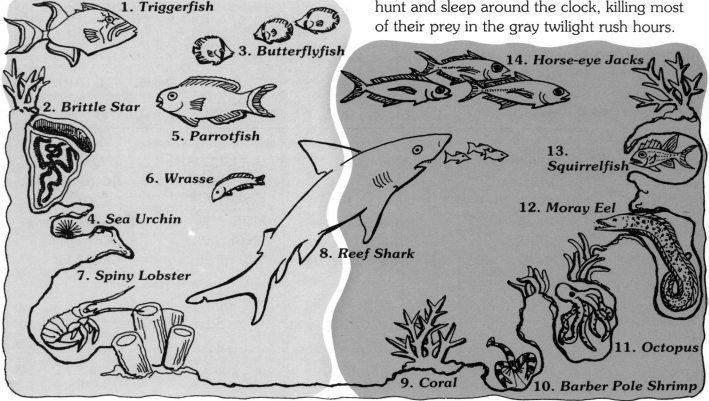

1. *Triggerfish*
3. *Butterflyfish*
2. *Brittle Star*
5. *Parrotfish*
6. *Wrasse*
4. *Sea Urchin*
7. *Spiny Lobster*
8. *Reef Shark*
14. *Horse-eye Jacks*
13. *Squirrelfish*
12. *Moray Eel*
11. *Octopus*
9. *Coral*
10. *Barber Pole Shrimp*

THE NIGHT SHIFT

At night, when a new crop of plankton fills the water, coral polyps come out of hiding and wave their tiny tentacles to catch the drifting plankton. Octopuses, which are shy during the day, boldly emerge from their lairs at night. Moray Eels wind their way among coral heads, Spiny Lobsters hunt snails and worms, sea urchins scrape algae from coral rocks, and Brittle Stars climb out of their sponge homes and scuttle quickly through the water. Barber Pole Shrimp take over the cleaning duties of daytime cleaners.

The fish that have been active during the day hover closer and closer to their coral homes until each one has nestled into a crevice to sleep. Some fish, such as parrotfish and surgeonfish, migrate in long caravans to their sleeping quarters. The parrotfish secrete their cocoons for protection during the night. Many fish put on "pajamas" to sleep in. That is, their bold daytime colors and markings fade, and they put on darker colors, pale blotches, and washes of red and brown. Their pajama colors help protect them from being seen by predators.

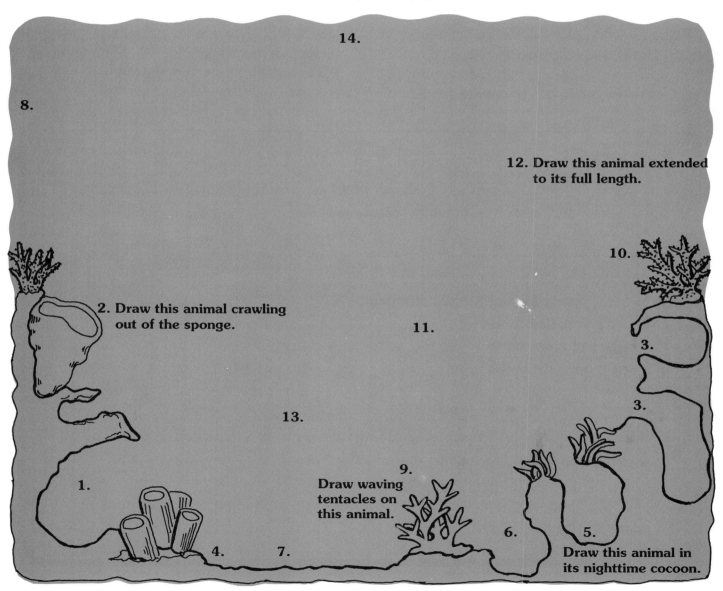

14.

8.

12. Draw this animal extended to its full length.

10.

2. Draw this animal crawling out of the sponge.

11.

3.

3.

13.

9.
Draw waving tentacles on this animal.

1.

6.

5.

4.   7.

Draw this animal in its nighttime cocoon.

REEF REPORT

I can't think of anything in the world more fun to explore than tide pools! When the tides ebb and flow over a rocky beach, little pools of water are trapped in pockets in the rocks. Each tide pool is like a separate world with its own ecosystem of tiny plants and animals.

One day when we were driving around the island—on the *left* side of the road, which is the custom in Grand Cayman—we took a sandy road to the ocean on the island's East End. The tide was low, and the rocky shore sparkled with the tide pools left behind.

We spent hours gazing into the clear pools, moving from one to another the way you move through the exhibits in a public aquarium. In fact, each tide pool *was* a natural aquarium featuring a different creature—a Sea Egg, a hermit crab, a Brittle Star, a neon-colored fish, a jellyfish, and a Feather Duster Worm.

The water in the tide pools was as clear as glass and perfectly still at this time of day during low tide. When the tide comes in, the pools are washed by rushing waves. Many of the animals and plants that live in tide pools have developed ways to cling to the rocks. The changing tides supply the pools with new food and clean water.

Tide pools can survive the assaults of winds and waves, but they are defenseless against humans. We must be gentle with them and resist the temptation to collect the little animals that live in them.

Try This! Make an Underwater Viewing Box!

Ask a parent or friend to help you make an underwater viewing box. Use it to explore tide pools or to look underwater when you go wading.

What You Will Need:
Four ¾" x 6" x 12" boards
Twelve aluminum six-penny nails, hammer
Exterior paint, paintbrush
12" square of clear acrylic
Silicone rubber caulking

To see underwater, place the acrylic bottom of the box just below the surface of the water. Don't let the box fill with water.

What to Do:
1. Nail the four boards together as shown above. Paint both sides of the wood with several coats of paint to make it waterproof.
2. Lay a bead of caulking completely around the bottom edge of the box. Then push the acrylic square gently into the caulking. Add caulking around the outside edges of the acrylic and in the corners.

WHAT'S IN A TIDE POOL?

Directions: In the illustration above, you can see some of the plants and animals that we found when we spent a day exploring tide pools. Look at the key to the illustration below, where each animal and plant is numbered. Then match each animal or plant described below with its correct number. The first one is done for you. *Answers are on page 63.*

Key to Illustration

__7__ **Red Rock Urchin**, a small sea urchin with black spines and a red **test** (the "shell" that covers the urchin's body).

____ **Feather Duster Worms** disappeared into their tubes when we drew near.

____ **Intertidal Chiton** has 8 plates across its back. It grips the tide pool rocks with a snail-like foot.

____ **Common Brown Algae** form miniature gardens of light brown and white "curls."

____ **Brittle Star** moves quickly like a snake, not stiffly like a sea star.

____ **Sea Egg**, a round sea urchin with white spines and a black test.

____ **Tessellated Nerite** has a white shell checked with black.

____ **Frillfin Goby,** a little fish with belly fins that join together into a sucker-like disk that keeps it from being swept out of the tide pool by waves.

REEF REPORT

The day finally came when we set out to swim with the stingrays! But first, our boat anchored in a twelve-foot-deep Turtle Grass bed where we were invited to dive for the beautiful Queen Conch shell. It's easy to take a large conch as it slowly looks for food along the sandy bottom. The conchs collected by the boat's passengers and crew would be cleaned and served for lunch, and the leftovers would be fed to the stingrays. I didn't take a conch. I didn't have the heart for it.

When I lived on Maui, I was an avid shell diver. I collected living shells and coral the way I picked wildflowers, with the same delight and irresponsible abandon. I acted as if these wild things were there for the taking. It was years before my generation realized its mistake.

Today we understand better that every living thing—whether it is a wildflower or a marine animal in a shell—needs to be cherished and protected. In the Caymans, as well as in many other countries, conchs are protected in Marine Parks and Replenishment Zones, and there are laws restricting the number that can be taken from other areas. Governments must constantly monitor the well-being of animal populations and wisely change the laws when they need to.

I have a beautiful collection of shells and coral, but I can't look at it without sadness and regret. I think your generation is more eco-smart than mine, and I believe you will take better care of the earth—because you *must*.

THE QUEEN CONCH

The Queen Conch is a large marine snail that lives in sandy areas where Turtle Grass grows. It produces a spiral shell with a bright pink lip. The Queen Conch slowly crawls across the sandy bottom on its muscular foot, withdrawing tightly into its shell if disturbed. The edible conch, which can be up to one foot long, is collected for food, as well as for its beautiful shell. The rosy shell is used to make cameos.

Queen Conchs are becoming scarce because so many people collect them to eat and to sell to tourists as souvenirs. What would be a better way to remember the reef? HINT:

A billion-dollar industry is built on collecting and selling thousands of tons of corals and ornamental shells worldwide. In Hawaii, tons of corals are harvested for commercial use. In Florida, it is against the law to collect corals, either alive or dead. The Queen Conch is a protected species in Florida, because it is nearly extinct in local waters. But even with stricter laws in place, many shells and corals are taken illegally. As long as there is a demand for these souvenirs of the coral reef, they will be collected. We must determine to take only pictures, not living animals!

As our boat left the conch beds behind, I knew we were finally heading for that unique area of the North Sound where stingrays play with people. Looking down into the clear, dazzling water, we began to see great dark shapes gliding beneath the boat.

I knew that Southern Stingrays can be dangerous. They have a single barb like a sharp serrated knife near the base of their powerful tails, and poison in the barb can cause pain, paralysis, or even death. But these stingrays have become tame enough to touch and feed by hand.

As soon as I entered the water, I was surrounded by stingrays, most of them about five feet across. Their **pectoral** fins are like wide wings that ruffle gracefully as they swim. They seemed to be performing a complicated dance, weaving over and under each other—and me! I dove down to swim with them and reached out to touch them. As close as we were, and although they often brushed against me, they kept their dangerous barbs in a safe position.

One of the boat crew lifted a baby stingray out of the water to show us its white underside. The little stingray squirted a spout of water from its mouth, making it look like a naughty child. I held out my arms and balanced the three-foot-wide animal just below the surface of the water, where it rested quietly. It felt rubbery and slippery and wonderful! How exciting to hold this curious underwater creature!

Although feeding and taming the stingrays has changed their normal behavior, an encounter of this kind helps many people become concerned for the first time about sea animals other than whales and seals. Swimming with stingrays gives us an unexpected feeling of kinship with one of the strange animals in the underwater world.

THE SOUTHERN STINGRAY

Southern Stingrays, which look like underwater birds with rippling wings, are really large fish. They often lie motionless on the ocean floor, covered with a layer of sand except for their eyes and gill openings. Normally, they are solitary, timid, and active at night, feeding on sand dwellers such as worms and crustaceans. Grand Cayman is

Swimming with stingrays was an extraordinary and rare experience never to be forgotten.

the only place in the world where rays congregate in groups, feed during the day, and seem to enjoy being with people. Apparently, feeding the stingrays and changing their natural behavior hasn't harmed them, and it has given researchers a chance to learn more about them.

THE IMPORTANCE OF THE CORAL REEF

Directions: Read the sentences below. Which do you think states the most important reason for protecting coral reefs? Put an X next to the one you choose. Then find out what your choice says about you.

What is the most important reason for protecting coral reefs?

_____ 1. The coral reef is a special place with an incredible diversity of animal life. It is home to many endangered and threatened species of marine wildlife.

_____ 2. The coral reef attracts visitors from all over the world who like diving, boating, fishing, and exploring nature. Tourist dollars support many local businesses and are often crucial to local economies.

_____ 3. As our world population continues to grow, we look to the oceans as an important source of food. Many edible marine species depend on healthy coral reefs for breeding and nursery grounds in order to survive.

_____ 4. Scientists are discovering how to make new agricultural, industrial, and medical products from marine organisms. The coral reef has yielded new medicines, foods, fertilizers, and **emulsifiers** used in industry.

_____ 5. When thriving coral reefs become distressed, it is a warning sign that something is critically wrong—something that will ultimately affect our own survival too. It alerts us to examine what we are doing to our air, water, and earth.

_____ 6. Reefs help protect tropical shores from erosion. Waves caused by tropical storms are weakened as they break on the reefs before reaching the shore.

What does your choice say about you?

1. If you chose the first reason, you are a nature lover. You know more about animals and plants than most of your friends do. You could help protect coral reefs by sharing what you know.
2. If you chose the second reason, you have a good mind for business. You could help protect coral reefs by raising funds for an environmental organization.
3. If you chose the third reason, you care about the basic needs of people. You could help protect coral reefs by writing letters to politicians and businessmen who make decisions that affect people's lives.
4. If you chose the fourth reason, you are a person who values science and technology. You could help protect reefs by coming up with a new idea for letting people know reefs are threatened.
5. If you chose the fifth reason, you "think big" and accept responsibility for actively caring for the earth. You could help protect coral reefs by taking practical steps in your own life, such as conserving resources and recycling.
6. If you chose the sixth reason, you are a practical person who respects the order and balance of nature. You could help others understand why coral reefs are important in the world.

THREATS TO THE CORAL REEF

Coral reefs have existed for millions of years. They have survived countless large and small changes in the environment. But today, coral reefs around the world are threatened as never before. Reefs in at least twenty countries, including the United States, Mexico, Indonesia, Japan, and Australia, are showing signs of stress and distress. Coral reefs in Florida are disappearing at an alarming rate. Coral diseases and **coral bleaching** occur when the water off Florida is no longer clear and clean, or when the water temperatures rise. In Hawaii, beautiful coral reefs have been damaged or killed by sewage pollution, dumped waste, or dredged mud. Many scientists agree that if the trend continues for another twenty or thirty years, there may not be any healthy coral reefs left on earth.

Directions: Read below about threats to coral reefs. Put an **N** next to the natural threats (caused by nature) and an **H** next to the human threats (caused by people). Which do you think are more dangerous to coral reefs—natural events or the activities of people? *Answers are on page 63.*

_____ **1.** Hurricanes and tropical storms break and topple coral and batter fish.

_____ **2.** Construction on or near the reef destroys coral or muddies the water, so that corals smother.

_____ **3.** Overfishing and destructive fishing methods (such as using dynamite, cyanide, bleach, fish traps, gill nets, or huge forty-mile-long drift nets) spoil the reef ecosystem.

_____ **4.** Too much rain dilutes the water, so that it isn't salty enough for corals.

_____ **5.** Marine debris is dangerous to corals, birds, sea turtles, fish, and other marine animals.

_____ **6.** Divers, snorkelers, and fishermen damage the reef with boats, anchors, and heavy gear. Even touching coral or standing on it can kill it.

_____ **7.** Changes in currents can smother corals in mud.

_____ **8.** Collecting tropical fish, corals, and shells strips the reef of life.

_____ **9.** Pollution from oil spills, chemical wastes, run-off from farms and factories, and sewage ruins the water quality that corals need.

_____ **10.** Natural predators, such as parrotfish, sponges, and sea urchins, eat corals or weaken it by boring into it.

_____ **11.** Warmer water caused by the greenhouse effect may cause coral bleaching, a dangerous condition that occurs when corals lose their algae partners.

Coral is often used in construction.

CAN YOU FIND 15 THREATS TO THE CORAL REEF?

Directions: Study the illustration on these two pages. Look for 15 threats to the coral reef and circle each one. *Check your answers on page 63.*

A thriving, healthy reef.   *A damaged, dying reef.*

WHAT CAN YOU DO?

Realize that what we do on land affects life in the sea.

Fight pollution by recycling, reusing, and reducing waste.

Watch how your family uses and disposes of pesticides, fertilizers, chemicals, cleaning products, motor oil, and paints.

Don't litter. Don't participate in balloon launches. Remember that anything can make its way to the ocean.

Never throw trash into the sea. Plastics and six-pack rings, especially, can kill marine animals. Participate in a Beach Cleanup. Pick up trash anytime you see it.

Learn more about coral reefs and share what you learn. Sponsor a reef awareness week in your school or community.

Write to decision makers in business and government. Support coral reefs, clean water, and marine sanctuaries.

Adopt a coral reef animal at your local zoo or aquarium.

Support environmental organizations that work to protect reefs.

Don't buy coral, coral jewelry, or shells. Do buy underwater photos or books and videos about the reef. You can collect pieces of dead coral and shells that wash up on the beach.

When you visit a coral reef, don't touch coral with your hands or feet. Wear a float-coat, so that you don't have to stand on the coral to rest or adjust your gear. Don't collect or bother any living thing. Don't feed fish. Obey all regulations.

REEF REPORT

Besides snorkeling, we enjoyed exploring the shore areas of Grand Cayman. On the south side of the island, there are blow holes that are great fun to watch. The waves come rushing in against the rocky shore, filling tunnels and crevices in the rocks and building up an enormous pressure. When the water is forced through holes in the ceilings of the rocks, it shoots up twenty or thirty feet in the air like water gushing from a fireman's hose.

We enjoyed the shore birds, too. My favorite reef "fisher-bird" is the mighty Frigate-bird, which is also called the Man-o'-War-bird. Its wingspan is almost eight feet! The black Frigate, with its powerful wings and scissor tail, soars and glides with easy grace as it hunts for fish. We watched a Frigate suddenly zoom down, pick up a large fish, eat it in the air, and continue fishing.

As we walked along the rocky beach, I filled a bag with a large collection—not of treasures but of trash. I picked up a Styrofoam sheet made of tiny pellets (deadly beads that could be eaten by fish and sea creatures) and several lengths of plastic cord and fishing line. Fish, birds, and other marine life can become tangled in discarded lines and injured. I picked up pieces of plastic, too, which may kill the animals that eat them.

I didn't collect all the trash I saw. It probably would have taken hours. But at least I tried to undo some of the mess that careless individuals had made. Sometimes we feel overwhelmed by how big environmental problems seem to be and we wonder, "What can one person do?" Well, one person can at least undo what one other person did. One person can encourage other people to act differently. And one person can get together with others and really make a difference. Remember, massive coral reefs are built by tiny individuals working together, and the structure they build sustains all the life on the reef.

A BEACH CLEANUP

We can't afford to litter, because we live on too small a planet. Wind and water can carry trash and poisonous wastes thousands of miles. Even if you live far from the ocean, litter from your area may end up in the sea. If your school or community holds a balloon launch—no matter how far inland you are—some of the balloons may come down on beaches or in the ocean. When sea turtles and other marine animals eat balloons, they often die. Try to think of a different way to enjoy balloons or a way to celebrate without them.

If you live near the ocean, participate in a Beach Cleanup or an Adopt-a-Beach program. Every year, during beach cleanups all over the world, people pick up tons of trash and save the lives of countless marine animals. To join a Beach Cleanup, write to:

The Center for Marine Conservation
1725 DeSales Street NW, Suite 500
Washington, DC 20036
(Or call **1-800-CMC-BEACH**)

REEF REPORT

On one of our last snorkeling trips, I was following a Queen Triggerfish, the most beautiful fish I have ever seen. I marveled at every detail of its coloring: it had a pink forehead and a pink smile stripe, a blue "moustache," teal and pink sides with each scale outlined in pink, an orange-yellow underside, a tail of gold and green and orange and blue, and sky blue fins.

Fighting a brisk current and holding an underwater camera with both hands, I took a deep breath and dove down to capture the triggerfish on film. As I was swimming back to the surface, I saw a man and woman underwater examining a fragile Elkhorn Coral. To my horror, the man broke off a large branch of living coral to show his companion.

After I surfaced, I looked for the couple again but I couldn't find them, so I have no way of knowing what they were thinking. Were they just being careless and cruel, or did they honestly not know that coral is a living animal? Some divers still believe that coral is some kind of inanimate rock.

The laws against touching or damaging coral, like laws against littering, are almost impossible to enforce. They must be self-enforced. Laws are an important part of protecting coral reefs, but individual attitudes, education, compassion, and caring are even more important.

Many scientists agree that seventy percent of the coral reefs on earth are threatened. Human beings have been the worst enemies of the reef, but we can learn how to be its friends. It is urgent that we begin now to cherish and protect the incredible coral reef.

Directions: Use the space below to write down some of your thoughts about the coral reef. Then share what you write with your family or friends.

MY THOUGHTS ABOUT THE CORAL REEF

Art Ideas to Help Save Coral Reefs

No matter where you live or what age you are or what resources you have, YOU can help protect coral reefs! One of the most important things you can do is something you are doing right now—learning all you can about coral reefs. The next thing is to share what you have learned. The more that people know about coral reefs, the more they will care about them and work to protect them.

Directions: Use the "Sea Art" on pages 52 and 53 to interest and inform others about coral reefs. Here are some ideas for using the art.

Make Posters, Note Cards, or Book Covers

Take every opportunity to show people how beautiful and interesting the coral reef community and its creatures are. Color the Sea Art with bright, gorgeous colors. Add your own art, too, to make coral reef designs for note cards, book covers, bookmarks, school reports, etc. Make posters with specific messages about how to protect coral reefs.

Make a T-Shirt with a Message

Create a design and a message for a T-shirt, so that every time you wear it, others will be reminded of the coral reef as a unique and wonderful community that needs to be protected. Use fabric paints to paint your design directly on the shirt. Or create your design on white paper with fabric crayons. To transfer the design onto the fabric, place it crayon-side down on a T-shirt that is 50% cotton and 50% polyester. Then put a plain sheet of paper on top of the paper with the design. Press with a hot iron until the color is transferred to the fabric.

Send a Postcard

Write letters to decision makers to let them know you care about coral reefs.

President _____
The White House
Washington, DC 20501

Senator _____
US Senate
Washington, DC 20510

Secretary General _____
United Nations
New York, NY 10017

To: _____

SEA ART AND . . .

Use the Sea Art on these pages to make projects that will teach others about the coral reef and alert them to its plight. See page 13, "Make a Magical Coral Reef," and page 51, "Art Ideas to Help Save Coral Reefs" for ideas. Of course, you will have lots of ideas of your own, too!

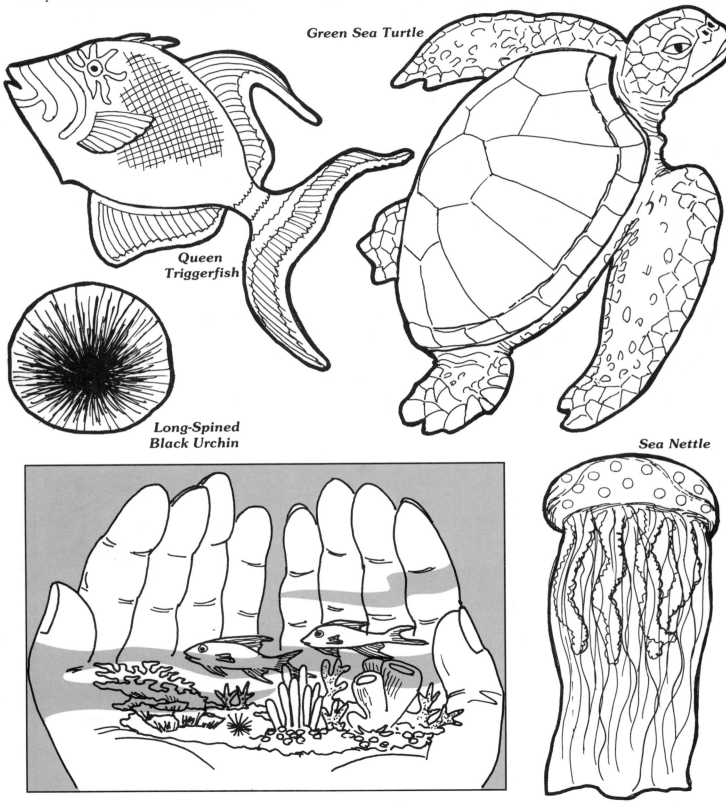

Green Sea Turtle

Queen Triggerfish

Long-Spined Black Urchin

Sea Nettle

...MORE SEA ART

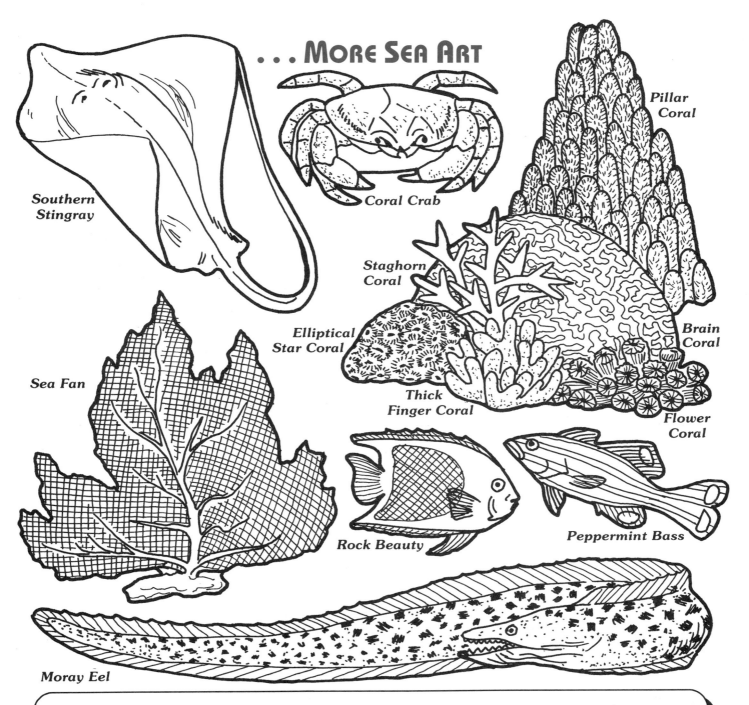

Southern Stingray

Coral Crab

Pillar Coral

Staghorn Coral

Elliptical Star Coral

Brain Coral

Sea Fan

Thick Finger Coral

Flower Coral

Rock Beauty

Peppermint Bass

Moray Eel

Try This! Make a Sun Catcher

Use the Sea Art to make a design on paper. Color it with bright markers and cut it out. Cut two frames (any shape) out of construction paper. Cut the same shape from a blue plastic report cover or from blue tissue paper or cellophane. Glue your design on the blue material. Then frame the design by gluing one frame on the front and one on the back. Hang the sun catcher in a window with a length of string.

VISIT A CORAL REEF EXHIBIT

You can learn about the coral reef from books, videos, and computer software, but the best way to appreciate the reef is actually to get your eyes on it! Even if you live thousands of miles from a living reef, you may be able to visit a coral reef exhibit at a zoo or aquarium or even at a tropical fish store. When you visit an exhibit, be a "Reef Spy."

HOW TO BE A REEF SPY

To be a Reef Spy, you must be keenly observant. Take time to look at details—at colors, patterns, textures, and movements. Watch a single fish or sea animal for a while to see what it is doing. Try to identify different kinds of coral. Read the information given at the exhibit. To see how you measure up as a Reef Spy, fill out the Reef Spy Observation Form below.

Directions: When you visit a coral reef exhibit, look for the things that are listed in the boxes below. As you find one of them, answer the question about it, and give yourself one point. At the end of your visit to the exhibit, add up your points to see what kind of Reef Spy you are.

14-16 Points:	**Nothing escapes you. You have the eye of a twilight predator.**
11-13 Points:	**You are a skilled observer. You can wear your Reef Spy diving gear proudly.**
6-10 Points:	**You'll be doing Tide Pool Patrol for a while longer.**
1-5 Points:	**You need to go to Reef Spy School.**

Reef Spy Observation Form

Sea Anemone: What color is it?	**Coral:** Is it living coral or artificial?	**Sea Urchin:** Where is it resting?	**Printed Information:** Write a fact.
Sponge: What is its shape?	**Fish With Stripes:** Name it.	**Fish With Spots:** Name it.	**Octopus:** What color is it?
Jellyfish: What is its size?	**Sea Fan:** Is it purple?	**Sea Star:** How many arms?	**Fish With 3 Colors:** Name it and its colors.
Sea Turtle: Is it endangered?	**Stingray:** Where is its mouth?	**Lobster:** What color is it?	**Shrimp:** What is it doing?

Try This!

Use the grid above to play "Reef Spy Bingo" when you visit a reef exhibit with a friend. Take turns finding an animal and answering the question about it. (Each of you should use a different colored pen.) Whoever fills in a horizontal or vertical row first wins.

CORAL REEF EXHIBITS

You'll have fun visiting a coral reef exhibit. Below is a partial list of marine centers, aquariums, and other places that have reef exhibits. Don't forget to take your Reef Spy Observation Form on page 54 when you go.

Aquarium of the Americas
New Orleans, LA 70130
(504) 861-2537

The Living Seas
EPCOT Center, Disney
    World
Orlando, FL 32830
(407) 560-7688

Henry Doorly Zoo
Omaha, NE 68107
(402) 733-8401

John C. Shedd Aquarium
Chicago, IL 60605
(312) 939-2426

Key West Aquarium
Key West, FL 33040
(305) 296-2051

Marineland of Florida
St. Augustine, FL 32086
(904) 471-1111

Marine World Africa
Vallejo, CA 94589
(707) 644-4000

Miami Seaquarium
Key Biscayne, FL 33149
(305) 365-2519

Mystic Marinelife
    Aquarium
Mystic, CT 06355
(203) 536-3323

National Aquarium
Baltimore, MD 21202
(410) 576-8685

New England Aquarium
Boston, MA 02110
(617) 973-5200

Quebec Aquarium
Quebec, Quebec, Canada
G1W 4S3
(418) 659-5264

Sea Life Park Hawaii
Waimanalo, HI 96795
(808) 259-8909

Seattle Aquarium
Seattle, WA 98101
(206) 386-4320

Sea World
San Diego, CA 92109
(619) 226-3939

Sea World of Florida
Orlando, FL 32821
(407) 351-3600

Sea World of Ohio
Aurora, OH 44202
(216) 562-8101

Steinhart Aquarium
San Francisco, CA 94118
(415) 750-7145

Stephen Birch Aquarium
Scripps Institution of
    Oceanography
La Jolla, CA 92037
(619) 534-FISH

Vancouver Aquarium
Vancouver, British Columbia,
Canada V6B 3X8
(604) 268-9900

Waikiki Aquarium
Honolulu, HI 96815
(808) 923-9741

HOW TO SNORKEL

What You Will Need:
- A mask
- A snorkel
- Fins
- Sunscreen
- A float-coat (optional)
- An underwater camera (optional)
- An underwater notebook (optional)

What to Do:

1. Buy, borrow, or rent your snorkeling gear. Make sure the fins fit comfortably. Check the fit of your mask by pushing it tightly against your face (without pulling the strap around your head). Breathe in through your nose to pull the mask against your face. Will the mask stay on your face for a moment without your holding it? Then it fits!

2. Use sunscreen or wear a T-shirt to protect your skin from the sun. But don't put sunscreen on your face or forehead.

3. Choose your dive buddy. NEVER SWIM ALONE.

4. Sit at the edge of the water or stand in shallow water to put on your gear. Put the mouthpiece of your snorkel in your mouth and clip the breathing tube to your mask, so that it is above water when your face is in the water. Put on your fins and float-coat. Now you're ready to go!

5. Swim slowly. Keep your face in the water and use the snorkel to breathe through your mouth. Use a dive flag to alert boats of your position in the water. Look around and marvel at what you see!

ATTENTION!
Learn to dive or snorkel safely by getting qualified instruction. Look in the Yellow Pages of the telephone book under "Diving Instruction."

Remember! You can snorkel anywhere you like to swim—in a creek, pond, or lake as well as the sea!

Assemble your gear. Wear a float-coat if you want extra support in the water.

You can buy a single-use underwater camera for around $20.00. It will give you twenty-four color prints.

You can even buy an underwater notebook. Or make your own underwater slate with a piece of Plexiglas® and a grease pencil. Then you can make notes while you are swimming!

Directions: After you go snorkeling, use this dive log to keep a record of your adventure. Or make up an adventure! You could write about encountering a killer shark, exploring a sunken submarine, or finding a fabulous underwater treasure.

DIVE LOG

Diver _____ **Date** _____

Dive Location _____

Dive Buddy _____

_____

_____

_____

_____

_____

_____

_____

_____

_____

_____

_____

_____

_____

_____

_____

_____

_____

_____

_____

_____

ENVIRONMENTAL ORGANIZATIONS

Some of the environmental organizations that are concerned about coral reefs are listed below. You can write to any of these organizations to learn more about coral reefs and about how you can help protect them.

Caribbean Conservation Corporation
PO Box 2866
Gainesville, FL 32602
(800) 678-7853

Center for Marine Conservation
1725 DeSales Street, NW, Suite 500
Washington, DC 20036
(202) 429-5609

Greenpeace
568 Howard Street, Third Floor
San Francisco, CA 94105
(415) 512-9025

Ocean Voice International, Inc.
PO Box 37026
3332 McCarthy Road
Ottawa, Ontario, Canada K1V 0W0
(613) 264-8986

Okeanos Ocean Research Foundation
431 East Main Street
Riverhead, NY 11901
(516) 369-9840

Reef Relief
Environmental Center and Store
201 William Street, PO Box 430
Key West, FL 33041
(305) 294-3100

The Cousteau Society
870 Greenbriar Circle, Suite 402
Chesapeake, VA 23320
(804) 523-9335

The Nature Conservancy
1815 North Lynn Street
Arlington, VA 22209
(703) 841-5300

The Star Thrower Foundation
PO Box 2200
Crystal River, FL 34423-2200
(904) 563-0022

World Wildlife Fund
1250 24th Street, NW
Washington, DC 20037
(202) 293-4800

Some Things to Remember When Writing a Letter
1. Write neatly.
2. Be specific.
3. Be courteous.
4. Include your return address.
5. Ask for a reply.

BOOKS ABOUT THE CORAL REEF

A Reef Comes to Life: Creating an Undersea Exhibit by Nat Segaloff and Paul Erickson. Franklin Watts, 1991.

A Walk on the Great Barrier Reef by Caroline Arnold. The Lerner Group, 1988.

Coral Reef by Michael George. Creative Education, 1992.

Coral Reef by Barbara Taylor. Dorling Kindersley, 1992.

Coral Reefs by Dwight Holing. Blake Publishing, 1990.

Coral Reefs by Lawrence Pringle. Simon & Schuster, 1995.

Coral Reefs by Alberto De Larramendi Ruis. Children's Press, 1993.

Coral Reefs by Jenny Wood. Garenth Stevens, 1991.

Coral Reefs in Danger by Christopher Lampton. Millbrook Press, 1992.

Corals: The Sea's Great Builders by Cousteau Society Staff. Simon & Schuster, 1992.

Crazy Tropical Fish Game. Price Stern Sloan, 1994.

Dentro del Arrecife de Coral (At Home in the Coral Reef) by Katy Muzik. Charlesbridge Publishing, 1993.

Exploring an Ocean Tide Pool by Jeanne Bendick. Henry Holt, 1992.

Great Barrier Reef by Martin J. Gutnik and Natalie Browne-Gutnik. Raintree Steck-Vaughn Publishers, 1994.

Inside Biosphere 2: The Ocean and Its Reef by Linnea Gentry. Biosphere Press, 1993.

Life in a Coral Reef by Melvin Berger. Newbridge Communications, 1994.

Make Your Own Coral Reef: Includes Giant Three-Dimensional Press-Out Model by Sue Wells. Dutton Children's Books, 1994.

Mangrove Wilderness: Nature's Nursery by Dianca Lavies. Dutton Children's Books, 1994.

Marine Tropical Fish by John Green. Dover Publications, 1994.

Night Reef: Dusk to Dawn on a Coral Reef by William Sargent. Franklin Watts, 1991.

Sand to Sea: Marine Life of Hawaii by Stephanie Feeney and Ann Fielding. University of Hawaii, 1989.

Scuba Diving by Bob Italia. Abdo & Daughters, 1994.

Snorkeling by Mike Holbrook. Silver Burdett Press, 1994.

Snorkeling for Kids by Judith Jennet. National Association of Underwater Instructors, 1992.

The Great Astrolabe Reef by Alexandra Siy. Silver Burdett Press, 1992.

The Great Barrier Reef: A Living Laboratory by Rebecca L. Johnson. Lerner Group, 1991.

The Hawaiian Coral Reef Coloring Book by Katherine Orr. Stemmer House Publishers, 1992.

THE INCREDIBLE CORAL REEF: ANOTHER ACTIVE-LEARNING BOOK FOR KIDS by Toni Albert. Trickle Creek Books, 1996.

The Ocean Book: Aquarium and Seaside Activities and Ideas for All Ages by Center for Marine Conservation Staff. John Wiley & Sons, 1989.

Tide Pool by Christiane Gunzi. Dorling Kindersley, 1992.

The Incredible Coral Reef

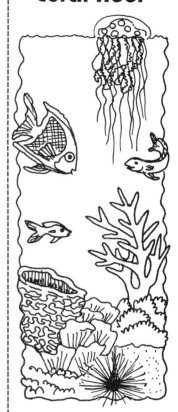

We must protect it!

Directions:
Color and cut out the bookmark to use when you read a book about the coral reef. You may want to glue the bookmark to heavy paper, so that it will last longer.

GLOSSARY

algae - a group of simple plants that often grow in colonies in water; most seaweeds are algae.

budding - a new coral polyp developing from an outgrowth, or "bud," on the original coral polyp.

camouflage - a natural disguise used for concealment.

carnivorous - feeding on animal flesh.

cleaners - small shrimp or fish that feed by cleaning parasites and unhealthy tissue from larger fish.

cleaning stations - the places on the reef where cleaning shrimp and fish make themselves available to clean parasites from larger fish.

clone - a group of individuals that are identical to their parent.

cocoon - a protective covering, or wrapping, produced by an animal. The mucus cocoon of a parrotfish is transparent.

colonial - living together in a group, or colony. Most corals are colonial; the coral polyps are physically connected to each other.

commensalism - a relationship between two species where one benefits and the other is neither benefited nor harmed. For example, an Urchin Crab lives and hides under the spines of the Long-spined Black Urchin. The Urchin Crab gains protection, but the sea urchin is not benefited or harmed.

coral bleaching - a dangerous condition that occurs when corals either reject their algae partners or the algae leave. The coral appears white, or "bleached," without the algae. Corals may die if they go too long without algae, although some bleached corals regain algae.

coral polyp - coral animal with a hollow body that is closed at one end; the mouth at the other end is surrounded by tentacles.

crustacean - an animal with a hard outer shell in the class Crustacea, which includes shrimps, crabs, and lobsters.

ecosystem - a community of animals and plants living in a certain environment. Together, they make up a unit in nature.

emulsifier - something that enables a mixture of liquids, such as oil and water, to form and be stable. The emulsifier enables very fine drops of one liquid to stay evenly scattered throughout the other.

equator - an imaginary circle around the middle of the earth, which is at an equal distance from the North and South Poles.

fore reef - the region seaward of the reef crest.

lagoon - a body of shallow salt water separated from the sea by a coral reef or bank.

mangrove - a tropical tree that sends out many prop roots. It grows in shallow salty water along sea coasts.

mucus coating - a thick, slimy substance secreted by many marine animals to provide a protective covering.

mutualism - a relationship between two species in which both benefit. For example, when a Snapping Shrimp and a goby share a burrow, the shrimp digs the burrow, giving the goby a place to hide, and the goby guards the burrow, alerting the shrimp to danger.

nematocysts - microscopic, stinging "darts" that line the tentacles of coral polyps and related animals.

niche - a habitat that supplies everything that a particular animal or plant needs in order to live.

nocturnal - active at night.

parasite - an animal or plant that benefits from living on or in another animal or plant; a parasite usually injures its host.

parasitism - a relationship between two species in which one benefits while the other is harmed. For example, when an isopod attaches itself to a fish, it feeds on the fish's blood, but the fish may be weakened or have tissue damage where the isopod is attached.

pectoral - in or on the chest. The pectoral fins of a fish correspond to the front legs of a four-legged animal.

phytoplankton - the mass of tiny plant life that floats in the ocean.

photosynthesis - the process by which a plant with chlorophyll makes food (sugars and starches) from water and carbon dioxide with energy from the sun.

planulae - "baby corals;" the tiny, oval larvae of corals.

pollutants - anything that pollutes, or contaminates.

predator - an animal that lives by killing and eating other animals.

prey - an animal hunted for food by another animal.

reef crest - the shallowest region of the reef, which is seaward of the lagoon.

shore zone - the region that is nearest the shore and includes the lagoon.

species - a group of plants or animals that are alike in certain ways and share a species name.

sperm - the male cells that fertilize eggs from the female to produce young.

supermale - a large agressive male fish, which was once a mature female fish. Supermales are often larger and more brilliantly colored than ordinary adult males.

symbiosis - a close, long-term relationship between two species living together. Mutualism, commensalism, and parasitism are kinds of symbiotic relationships.

test - an outer shell-like covering of many marine invertebrates, such as sea urchins.

tropical - the region of the earth that is between the Tropic of Cancer and the Tropic of Capricorn, noted for its hot climate.

zooplankton - the mass of tiny animal life that floats in the ocean. Both phytoplankton and zooplankton are primary links in the undersea food chain.

zooxanthellae (prounounced *zo-a-zan-THEL-a*) - single-celled algae that live in the tissues of corals and some other organisms.

ANSWERS

Page 9, "Or All Three?"
1. The algae living inside the coral polyp needs sunshine in order to make food through photosynthesis. **2.** Much of the color of coral comes from the zooxanthellae inside it. **3.** Symbiosis, or to be more specific, mutualism.

Page 12, "Consider the Kinds"
1. Giant Brain Coral. **2.** Thick Finger Coral. **3.** Flower Coral. **4.** Boulder Coral. **5.** Staghorn Coral.

Page 15, "The Coral Reef Eco-System"
1. D **a.** Mangrove swamp **b.** Seagrass bed **c.** Coral reef

Page 20, "Artificial Reefs"
Is This a FISH TALE? No, it's true! A new reef growing on an oil rig may be threatened by oil spills. Other reefs develop on structures that won't last thousands of years the way a natural reef does.

Page 21, "The Reef Connection"

Page 25, "The Reef Is Riddled with . . . RIDDLES"
1. A Star Coral. **2.** Because he was a Boring Sponge. **3.** A Brain Coral. **4.** An Octopus (Octo-puss). **5.** A Jellyfish. **6.** A Sea Fan. **7.** A Pillow Stinking Sponge. **8.** A Hermit Crab.

Page 26, "Just the Two of Us"
Is This a FISH TALE? No, it's true! A cleaner shrimp will tug at the tiny hairs on the back of a diver's hand and look for parasites.

Page 27, "More Twosomes"
1. a **2.** c

Page 28, "Hermits That Aren't Hermits"
3. a **4.** b

Page 30, "The Reef Is a Puzzle"

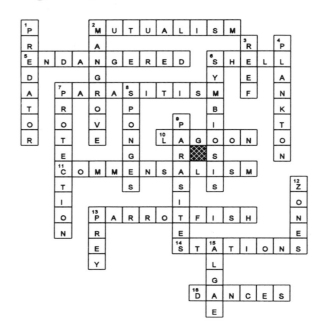

Page 37, "Words of Warning"

Message: Since all parts of the reef are connected, the destruction of even one part can cause a complete change in the entire reef.

Page 41, "What's in a Tide Pool?"
7. Red Rock Urchin **3.** Feather Duster Worms **8.** Intertidal Chiton **6.** Common Brown Algae **4.** Brittle Star **2.** Sea Egg **1.** Tessellated Nerite **5.** Frillfin Goby

Page 45, "Threats to the Coral Reef"
1. N **2.** H **3.** H **4.** N **5.** H **6.** H **7.** N **8.** H **9.** H **10.** N **11.** H
The activities of people are the major cause of destruction to coral reefs.

Pages 46-47, "Can You Find 15 Threats to the Coral Reef?"
1. A dredge is breaking coral underwater. **2.** The dredge is stirring up a dark silt runoff. **3.** A sea turtle is about to eat a plastic bag. **4.** An underwater photographer is standing on a coral. **5.** A sponge is boring into a coral. **6.** A parrotfish is eating coral. **7.** A tangled fishing line is sawing into a coral. **8.** A boat anchor is breaking a coral. **9.** Waste is running into the ocean from a factory. **10.** A diver is spearfishing. **11.** A fish is tangled in a plastic six-pack ring. **12.** A diver is breaking coral with his fins. **13.** The diver is collecting a shell. **14.** Dangerous trash is dumped in the ocean. **15.** A diver is using bleach to force a lobster out into the open.

CAN YOU FIND 15 THREATS TO THE CORAL REEF?

Directions: Study the illustration on these two pages. Look for 15 threats to the coral reef and circle each one. *Check your answers on page 63.*

Page 46   © Trickle Creek Books

© Trickle Creek Books   Page 47

Some Things to Think About

"While scuba diving in the Caribbean, I have seen and touched the white bones of a dead coral reef. . . In the last few years, scientists have been shocked at the sudden occurrence of extensive worldwide bleaching episodes from which increasing numbers of coral reefs have failed to recover. Though dead, they shine more brightly than before, haunted perhaps by the same ghost that gives spectral light to an elephant's tusk."

Vice President Al Gore in
Earth in the Balance, 1992

Besides being white, how is a bleached coral reef like the ivory tusk of an elephant? (Think about the condition of coral reefs—and of elephants—in today's world.)

"I believe in the forest, and in the meadow, and in the night in which the corn grows."

"Methinks my own soul must be a bright invisible green."

Henry David Thoreau in *A Plea for Captain John Brown* [1859]
and ***A Week on the Concord and Merrimack Rivers* [1849]**

Henry David Thoreau wrote about his love for nature. Can you find out what unusual thing he did to learn more about living with nature? Why do you think Thoreau imagined his soul as being bright green? What color do you associate with your own identity and individuality?

"The conquest of the earth is not a pretty thing when you look into it too much."

Joseph Conrad in *The Heart of Darkness* [1902]

Make a list of examples of modern progress, such as cars, shopping malls, and sprawling cities. Then decide which things on your list are harmful to the environment. Make a note next to each one, such as "not harmful," "causes pollution," "destroys wildlife habitat and trees," etc. Do you agree or disagree that "the conquest of the earth is not a pretty thing"? Is there anything we can do to make it prettier?